MW00466676

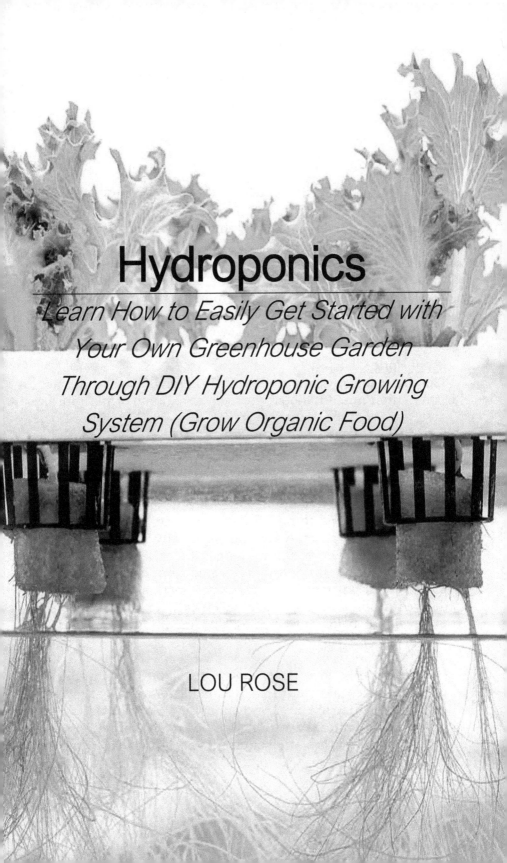

Hydroponics

Learn How to Easily Get Started with Your Own Greenhouse Garden Through DIY Hydroponic Growing System (Grow Organic Food)

LOU ROSE

Table of Contents

Introduction

The words "hydroponics" and "above ground" cultivators have and are still used to denote the same cultivation method, but in this text the word "hydroponics" is used when crop systems are purely hydroponic, that is - to say that there is no rooting medium or is considered that the rooting medium is inert. The word "above ground" is used for crop systems that are associated with crop production in which the environment can interact with the roots of plants, such as organic matter such as peat and pine bark. In plant-based biological technology, two words are often used: food and nutrients. It can be confusing if these words are not clearly defined and understood. In the 1950s, the word food used to identify chemical fertilizer, a substance containing one or more essential plant elements, became a common word.

Today, it is not uncommon in agricultural and horticultural literature to identify NPK fertilizer (nitrogen, phosphorus, potassium) as plant food, a combination of words that is generally accepted and common. The dictionary definition of plant-related foods is "inorganic substances that plants absorb in gaseous form or in aqueous solution" (Merriam Webster's Collegiate Dictionary, 10th ed., 1994). This definition in the dictionary would be in line with the word combination of plant foods, because chemical fertilizers are inorganic and the root absorption of the elements in chemical fertilizers takes place in an environment of aqueous solution. Consequently, the words food and / or plant foods would not refer to organic substances intended to be used as fertilizer, since these two terms are already defined to identify inorganic substances.

Therefore, these organic substances intended for use as fertilizer should be identified by name and not as food or vegetable food. The word nutrient is unclear in its meaning and is used in many different scientific fields. The definition of a dictionary does not help because it is not specific because it is defined as "nutrient or ingredient". For use in plant nutrition, nutrients are one of the thirteen basic plant mineral elements that are divided into two categories: six major mineral elements - N, P, K, Ca, Mg and S - are found in percentage concentrations in plant dry matter. and seven micronutrients - B, Cl, Cu, Fe, Mn, Mo and Zn - are found in plant dry matter at levels below 100% (see pp. 35-37).

To designate one of the thirteen basic essential mineral elements in a plant, the term vegetable nutrient is often used, for example to indicate that P is an essential nutrient for the plant. The use of the term nutrient does not give accurate identification as a link to plants. Unfortunately, the terminology used in scientific and technical journals on plants has been inconsistent in identifying essential plant mineral elements, calling them essential nutrients, plant nutrients, or simply the word nutrients.

For those in the plant sciences, they generally understand what these terms mean, but for someone who is not so engaged, the word nutrient could be used to refer to a wide variety of substances as "a nutrient or ingredient." the word nutrient is used as a comprehensive term to include organic compounds containing combined and bound carbon, hydrogen and oxygen. Therefore, one might ask: "What is the difference between a mineral vegetable and a substance identified as a nutrient that is an organic substance?" (Parker 1981; Landers 2001) It is difficult to answer this question because the criteria for determining the essentiality of mineral elements in vegetables have already been established (Arnon and Stout 1939; see p. 34), while the criteria for essentiality for elements other than mineral elements were absent.

Therefore, as with the use of the word food or plant food, the use of the word nutrient should be limited to the identification of the mineral element which is necessary for plants; those who suggest a plant nutrient for an organic substance should only use the word for that substance and not identify it as a nutrient.

Chapter 1: What is hydroponics?

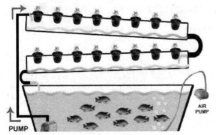

Hydroponics is the science of growing landless plants. If you haven't heard of hydroponics, you may have heard of "soil-less culture", which is another name often used to describe the same thing. The same natural elements necessary for plant growth in soils are used, but your plants are not limited by weeds or pests and diseases that transmit the soil.

Hydroponic techniques, although they may seem like a new technology that have been used for centuries. The earliest known uses of hydroponics were the Hanging Gardens of Babylon, the Kashmiri Floating Gardens, and the inhabitants of the Aztecs of Mexico who used rafts on shallow lakes to grow plants. In addition, hieroglyphic records in Egypt dating back hundreds of years BC describe the cultivation of plants in water. More recently, mobile hydroponic farms were used to feed soldiers during the Second World War in the South Pacific.

Today, hydroponics is starting to play a more important role in global agricultural production. Growing populations, climate change, water scarcity in certain regions or poor water quality are all factors that influence the trend towards alternative gardening methods. Hydroponics allow many to have fresh food where they would normally deliver or store it for long periods of time. The best example of this is the Navy submarines, where hydroponics is used to provide the crew with fresh fruits and vegetables. The use of hydroponics in developing countries is more useful, as it allows intensive production of food in limited areas. The only limitation of a sustainable hydroponic system is the availability of water and nutrients. In areas where fresh water is not available, desalinated seawater can be used.

Hydroponic gardening has been used commercially since the 1970s, although it has only recently become more popular with hobby growers. Community demand for ecological and healthy products is a major factor in this trend. By growing plants in a hydroponic system, you will know exactly what has entered the plants and you can ensure that no harmful pesticides are used that can harm your own health and that of the environment.

The process of hydroponic agriculture in our oceans dates back to the time of the creation of the Earth. Hydroponic farming preceded the cultivation of the soil. But as an agricultural asset, many believe that it started in the ancient city of Babylon with its famous hanging gardens. They are listed as one of the Seven Wonders of the Ancient World and were probably one of the first successful attempts to grow hydroponic plants.

Most of the greenhouse vegetable production in developed countries is done through the hydroponic system. Research at the Tree Research and Development Center in Harrow, Ontario, has resulted in a patented computer program called the Tree Manure Manager that controls the flow of nutrients to greenhouse plants.

Is hydroponics a science?

This test was repeated several times with no positive response. Most word references do not characterize hydroponics as a science, but rather another method for the development or development of plants. Nevertheless, Webster's New World College Dictionary, fourth edition (1999), defines hydroponics as "the study of the development or creation of plants in addition to a rich arrangement". I would expect the scientific perspective to be linked to the "rich arrangement supplement". Not even in the Wikipedia definition (www.wikipedia.com), and if hydroponics doesn't show "science". Presumably, the main association is actually occupied by a scientific angle by the National Aeronautical Space Administration (NASA), because a kind of hydroponic culture will be the strategy chosen to develop plants in space or on celestial bodies. Merriam Webster's definition of college vocabulary for science is "something (like a game or strategy) that could be considered or learned as systematized information." Hydroponics is certainly a process of plant development and it has collected a lot of information regarding plant development using the hydroponics technique (or should it be a hydroponics strategy?), Corresponding to the rule according to which "science" is given in the previous definition. In addition, there is a collection of "systematic data" which corresponds to the second part of the scientific definition.

Chapter 2: History of hydroponics

 You may have seen some types of soilless plants growing anywhere in movies or books and treated them like a science fiction story. However, this practice (called hydroponics) has been used for thousands of years.

The famous Babylonian hanging gardens, around 600 BC, are the first records of hydroponics.

Hanging garden of babylon

These gardens were built along the Euphrates in Babylonia. Because the climate in the region was dry and rarely seen rain, people believe that the ancient Babylonians used a chain traction system to water their garden plants.

In this method, the water withdrew from the river and poured down the chain system and descended to the steps or the ground floor of the garden.

Other records of hydroponics in ancient times have been found with floating farms around the island town of Tenochtitlan by the Aztecs in Mexico in the 10th and 11th centuries. And at the end of the 13th century, researcher Marko Polo noted in his writings that he had seen similar floating gardens during a trip to China.

Chronology of modern hydroponic development

It was not until 1600 that scientific experiments on the growth and constituents of plants were recorded. The Belgian Jan Van Helmont indicated during his experience that plants draw substances from water. However, he did not know that plants also needed carbon dioxide and oxygen from the air.

John Woodward monitored plant growth using water cultivation in 1699. He found that plants grow best in the water with the most soil. So he came to the conclusion that some of the substances in the water came from the soil, which caused the plants to grow, not the water itself.

In 1804, De Saussure suggested that plants consist of chemical elements absorbed by water, soil and air. Boussignault, a French chemist, then verified this proposal in 1851. He experimented with growing plants in an insoluble artificial medium, including sand, quartz, and landless charcoal. He only used water, mediums and chemical nutrients. And he found that plants needed water and got hydrogen from it; Plant dry matter contains hydrogen plus carbon and oxygen from the air; plants are made up of nitrogen and other mineral nutrients.

1860 and 1861 marked the end of a long search for the sources of nutrients necessary for the cultivation of plants when two German botanists Julius von Sachs and Wilhelm Knop delivered the first standard formula for the nutrients dissolved in the water in which the plants could grow, this is the origin "Nutriculture".

Today it is called water culture. With this method, the plant bark was completely immersed in an aqueous solution containing the minerals nitrogen (N), phosphorus (P), potassium (K), magnesium (Mg), sulfur (S) and calcium (Ca). Macronutrients or macronutrients are now visible (elements required in relatively large quantities).

However, it is surprising that the method of growing plants in water and nutrient solution is only considered as experiments and only used in a laboratory for plant research.

It was not until the greenhouse industry appeared that interest in the application of nuclear practice appeared in 1925. Researchers were concerned with the problems of soil cultivation methods with soil structure, fertility and pests. They worked intensively to reap the fruits of vegetable production in extensive agricultural production.

In the early 1930s, W.F. Gericke of the University of California at Berkeley experimented with cultivation to produce crops. He originally called this process aquaculture, but abandoned it after learning that the term was used to describe the culture of aquatic organisms.

The university still doubted his story of successful cultivation and asked two other students to investigate his request. The two investigated and reported their findings in a 1938 agricultural bulletin "A method of growing water to grow plants without soil".

They confirmed the use of hydroponics, but concluded their research that crops grown with hydroponics are no better than those grown on quality soils. However, they missed the many benefits of hydroponics in farming over cultural practices. The benefits that all hydroponic growers know by heart today. In the early 1930s, W.F. Gericke of the University of California at Berkeley experimented with cultivation to produce crops. He originally called this process aquaculture, but abandoned it after learning that the term was used to describe the culture of aquatic organisms.

The university still doubted his story of successful cultivation and asked two other students to investigate his request. The two investigated and reported their findings in a 1938 agricultural bulletin "A method of growing water to grow plants without soil".

They confirmed the use of hydroponics, but concluded their research that crops grown with hydroponics are no better than those grown on quality soils. However, they missed the many benefits of hydroponics in farming over cultural practices. The benefits that all hydroponic growers know by heart today.

The first known application of hydroponic plant selection occurred in the early 1940s when hydroponics were used on Wake Island, a landless island in the Pacific. The island served as a supply stop for American American companies. The lack of soil meant that it was impossible to cultivate using the cultivation method and that it was incredibly expensive to have fresh aerated vegetables. The hydroponics passionately solved the problems and supplied fresh vegetables to entire troops on this remote island.

Chapter 3: General hydroponics

 You may be wondering what is so specific to the brand and why all the noise surrounds it. General Hydroponics is the colloquial name for a range of quality products that provide complete nutrition for soil and hydroponic systems.

Plants require that there are all the conditions necessary to grow their growth. And it is your duty as a responsible farmer to secure them. Hydroponic systems are soilless systems. This means that they will need some sort of nutrient layer that contains the minerals necessary for healthy growth.

Using a hydroponic fertilizer that contains a full dose of nutrients for your garden is not a bad idea. This saves you a lot of stress and time spent in the garden and in the shop. And let's not forget a few extra dollars; when you're done with a lower quality product.

Why general hydroponics?

General Hydroponics has a complete nutrient solution for plants. no matter if you have soil or a hydroponic system, you want a bountiful harvest at the end of the growing season. This is why you want to feed your plants with the nutrients necessary for healthy growth. This brand contains all the nutrients you need.

If you're still having trouble deciding if this is the right product for you, here are some reasons to consider

Supports hydroponic systems

It can be very difficult to find the right blend for your hydroponic system. Here, the nutrients from hydroponic soil cultivation are generally considered to be better than other products. A wide range of products is designed to support all hydroponic systems.

General soil nutrients for hydroponic soil cultivation

It contains all the nutrients

A wide range of products is designed to provide your plant with all the nutrients it needs. It contains primary, secondary and complete micronutrient ingredients necessary for increased yield and better crop quality. Plants need phosphorus, potassium and magnesium to be available in the soil system. Other elements found in this product include nitrogen, calcium and sulfur. This is just as important for healthy plant development.

Easy to use

It's easy to apply different product offerings. You don't have to worry about using it. The mixtures easily adapt to the needs of your plant. You can easily improve the taste, aroma and nutrition by simply following the instructions on the product.

The pH of the mixture is correctly balanced. So you don't have to worry about getting it wrong or correcting General Hydroponics' soil nutrient formulation is one of the reasons why NASA and many other reputable research institutes use it.

Works on too much soil

Generally, the nutrients from hydroponics are also designed for use in soil gardening. This means that you can easily add the mixture to your lawn and garden for rapid growth. Can also be used in pots.

All organic ingredients

All General Hydroponics products are made from natural minerals and botanical extracts. This means you don't have to worry about added chemicals that can be toxic to your plants and the environment. There is growing concern about the safety of using fertilizers in the garden.

Chapter 4: Benefits hydroponic food production

1. No soil required

In a sense, you cultivate in places where the land is scarce, non-existent or heavily polluted. In the 1940s, hydroponics were successfully used to supply fresh vegetables to Wake Island troops, a supply point for American airlines. It is a highly cultivated area in the Pacific. In addition, hydroponics was considered by NASA to be the culture of the future, which will produce food for astronauts in space (where there is no ground).

2. Make better use of space and location

Because everything the plants need is secure and maintained in the system, you can grow in your small apartment or in guest rooms as long as you have space.

Plant roots are usually enlarged and developed in search of food and oxygen in the soil. This is not the case for hydroponics, where the roots sink into a container filled with oxygenated nutrient solution and come into direct contact with vital minerals. This means that you can grow your plants a lot more and save a lot of space.

3. Climate control

As in greenhouses, hydroponic producers can have complete control over the climate - temperature, humidity, light amplification, air composition. In this sense, you can grow food all year round, whatever the season. Farmers can produce food at the right time to maximize their commercial benefits.

4. Hydroponics save water

Plants grown in hydroponics can only use 10% water compared to field cultivation. Water is recirculated in this method. Plants will absorb the necessary water, while this runoff will be captured and returned to the system. Water loss occurs in only two forms - evaporation and leakage (but an effective hydroponic configuration minimizes or will have no leakage).

It is estimated that American agriculture uses up to 80% of ground and surface water.

Although water will become a critical problem in the future when food production is expected to increase by 70% according to the FAQ, hydroponics is considered a viable solution for large-scale food production.

5. Efficient use of nutrients

In hydroponics, you have 100% control over the nutrients (food) that plants need. Before planting, growers can check what plants need and the amounts of nutrients they need at certain stages and mix them with water accordingly. The nutrients are stored in the container, so there is no loss or change of nutrients like in the soil.

6. Ph control of the solution

All minerals are found in water. This means that you can measure and adjust the pH level of your water mixture much more easily than soil. This guarantees optimal absorption of nutrients in plants.

7. Better growth rate

Do hydroponic plants grow faster than in the ground? Yes it is.

You are the boss who manages the whole environment for the growth of your plants - temperature, light, humidity and above all nutrients. Plants are placed in ideal conditions, while nutrients are provided in sufficient quantity and come into direct contact with the root systems. In doing so, plants no longer consume precious energy by looking for diluted nutrients in the soil. Instead, they focus on growing and producing fruit.

8. No weeds

If you grew up in the soil, you will understand how irritating weeds cause your garden. This is one of the most difficult tasks for gardeners - wharf, plow, hoe, etc. Weeds are mainly associated with the soil. So, remove the soil and any weed rot will go away.

9. Fewer pests and diseases

And like weeds, removing soil helps make your plants less vulnerable to pests that carry soils like birds, pigeons, ground dogs; and diseases such as Fusarium, Pythium and Rhizoctonia. In addition, when grown indoors in a closed system, gardeners can easily take control of most of the surrounding variables.

10. Less use of insecticides and herbicides

Because you do not use the soil and weeds, pests and plant diseases are significantly reduced, less chemicals are used to help you grow cleaner, healthier food. Cutting insecticides and herbicides is a strong point of hydroponics when the criteria of modern life and food security are increasingly set.

Chapter 5: Build your own hydro systems

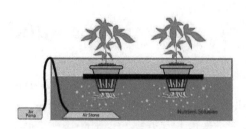

As prices vary from place to place, your exact cost will determine what you can get in your area. But you should have a four plant drip system to grow large plants to get all the supplies you need for less than $ 100. I built this system myself between $ 60 and $ 80. You may already have the necessary supplies in the house.

Although this system is designed to grow 4 plants in 5-gallon buckets, you can easily adapt it to grow more or less plants as desired, as well as in containers and buckets larger or smaller.

List of system parts used to build hydro systems

- 4 planters (for plants)
- 4 through holes (also called partitions)
- The black vinyl pipes (for fill and drain pipes) as well as the blue vinyl pipes from the hydroponic store will also work.
- 1 submersible fountain pump (present in most nursery)
- 18 to 30 gallons of tote (bigger is better in the long run)

- Hydronic growth medium (for plant support and moisture retention for roots)
- A cheap oven filter (to prevent the substrate from entering the tube)
- Several "T" fittings which correspond to the vinyl pipes you are using (how much depends on the final configuration)
- Two cans of cheap black spray paint and two cans of cheap white spray paint (to prove the light from the bins and tank)
- (Optional) Small quantity of PVC pipes and fittings (for return ends)

Additional items you need to grow

- Hydroponic nutrients (of any kind, as long as they exist for hydroponic plants).
- The pH Test Kit (pH Test Nutrient Solution) Lowering pH by General Hydroponics works best and is the cheapest way.
- PH adjusters (low pH and low pH) This involves adjusting the pH as needed after testing it.

In addition to hydroponic nutrients, pH test kits, pH adjustments and culture media, you should also be able to get the rest of the supplies you need from local stores such as Home Depot, Lowe's Wal-Mart, Target, Big lot, Kmart, etc. I received a deposit of five gallon buckets for about $ 2.50 and an 18-gallon warehouse at Wal-Mart for $ 3.50. I got the black vinyl fountain pump used for hydroponic pipes and "T" fittings at Lowe's.

The fountain pump also came from Lowe's. It was the most expensive part of the whole system. The pump costs around $ 40, but for this system you don't need a pump that big to get the job done, but it does allow you to expand the system in the future. Just make sure that each pump you use has a removable filter, and if not, you will do one to preserve the impurities.

Bulkhead openings / joints are available in all sizes and shapes. They are used in all industrial products, but most home improvement stores carry them somewhere in the store and are very likely to have them in multiple places. I bought them from the Home Depot electrical service for $ 1.97 api, right next to the electric tube.

You need to make sure that the end of the through hole on which the vinyl pipe runs (end without thread and nuts) will fit the size of the pipe you are using. Those in the photos above will accommodate 5/8 inch diameter tubes. Alternatively, you can use two hoses and / or a hose clamp to tighten. Or by cutting a small piece of pipe (the size corresponding to a through hole) and pushing it through the passage, then lowering the smaller pipe inside a larger one. If this is the case, you can use a small amount of waterproof adhesive between two different sizes and / or a hose clamp to make sure there is a waterproofing compound. You may also find that the old garden hose will fit perfectly and can be replaced with a vinyl hose for the return lines (drainage).

Cutting Hole for Holes the first step is to see the side of the hole through the thread and nut at the bottom of the 4 5-gallon buckets. You will need to be near the edge of the bucket, but not so close that you will not be able to install the nut to be able to install it (approximately one inch). This will allow you to stand it on a table or bench, and most of the weight of the bins will still be supported and will not tip over.

It is important not to make the holes too large, as they can leak. It must be large enough to retract the threaded side of the passage through without significant play.

Chapter 6: Hydro media & supplies

There are many types of breeding media that have been used successfully for hydroponics, and there are probably many others that have never been tried.

Some are:

1. Perlite - A gray obsidian volcanic rock that is heated to 1500 degrees F in the oven and expanded. It is a light porous material which can "eject" water from the bottom of the water tank.

2. Ceramic rock grows - a clay material also called geolite, which is often used in aquaculture because the porous material is a good way of growing bacteria for water purification. It does not collapse.

3. Rock wool - a material made of rock wrapped in fibrous material. Phenol-based resin is added as a binder. Rock wool also tends to increase the pH of water.

4. Pea Gravel - This medium is just plain gravel, but it is valued in size and shape. It is not a porous medium, so it does not empty the water from the bottom and must be used in a system allowing to ventilate the water. It can be used to grow bacteria as well as plants.

There are many other types of media used in hydroponic systems. Some have particular advantages and disadvantages.

Sand - Many sands, such as beach sand, are already in the media, which can cause hydroponic problems.

However, sand is a useful medium that retains water. It must be sterilized between cultures.

Sawdust - When wood production is high, sawdust may be available. Tree species are important and softwood decomposes more slowly than hardwood. Western deer and hedgehog dishes work very well, but red cedar is poisonous to plants. Part of the sawdust comes from logs soaked in salt water and is therefore toxic to plants.

Peat - There are three types of peat: peat moss, cane stool, and peat humus. Peat is very acidic and can lower the pH of nutritious water. It decomposes after one or two growing seasons.

Vermiculite - This is a volcanic silt that exploded in an oven. It is a magnesium aluminum silicone material which can be compressed and lose its porosity.

Plum - Silicone of volcanic origin can decompose after repeated use.

No media - There are many hydroponic systems that use no media. The plant is usually thrown in a small piece of rock wool or a specially designed plastic necklace. The plant is then placed in a growing tube or container that puts nutritious water into the roots.

There are probably hundreds of different types of plants to grow, and anything a plant can grow is considered a growth agent. There are artificial and organic (natural) environments. Even old plain AIR can be an effective root growth environment.

I have been asked many times which average crop is best. It's like asking what is the best color? Or what is the best type of vehicle you have. Sometimes the answer depends on the work you need to do. You would not try to use a soilless mix in the Aeroponic system and do not plow the field with a Rolls Royce sedan. However, if you want to build a hydroponic system that doesn't recover, then a soy-free mix would be a great choice, and a John Deere tractor can cultivate the field (except Rolls for a night in town, pick me up at 8), which what I mean is that the best culture the medium used depends on many variables. The type of system you use, the type of crop you grow and the local environment are just some of the deciding factors involved in selecting your plants to grow. There may be several media that will also work well for your particular needs. Often it depends on availability, price or personal preferences.

These are the popular mediums below:

The cubes oases

These light preformed cubes are designed for reproduction. A very popular medium for growing from seeds or cuttings. This product has a neutral pH and retains water very well.

The cubes are intended for starter supports and are available in three sizes up to 2 "x 2". They can be easily transplanted into almost any type of hydroponic system or medium (or soil).

Coconut fibers

Coconut fibers are quickly becoming one of the most popular growing media in the world. In fact, it may soon be the most popular. The first is a fully "organic" reproductive medium that offers superior performance in hydroponic systems. Coconut fibers are essentially the waste of the coconut industry, they are powdered coconut shells.

There are many advantages - it maintains a higher oxygen capacity than rock wool and has a higher capacity to retain water from rock wool, which is a real advantage for hydroponic systems which have intermittent watering cycles.

Coconut fibers are also rich in hormones that stimulate the root and provide some protection against root diseases, including fungal infections. Dutch producers have discovered that a blend of 50% coconut fiber and 50% expanded clay granules is the perfect breeding ground.

A word of warning on coconut fiber, you should be careful when buying coconut fiber. There is a generally lower level of coconut fiber which contains excellent sea salt and which is very fine grain. The lower quality coconut fiber will lead to disappointing results when used in a hydroponic system.

Perlite

Good old perlite! It has been around for years, mainly used as an additive to increase aeration and drainage of the soil. Perlite is an extracted material, a form of volcanic glass that heats up quickly to over 1600 degrees. f. it looks a bit like popcorn when the water evaporates and creates a myriad of tiny bubbles.

Perlite is one of the best hydroponic growing media around. It is used alone or in admixture with other agents. Perlite is most commonly used with vermiculite (a combination of 50 to 50 is a very popular medium) and is also one of the main ingredients in a salt-free mixture. perlite has a good wicking action which makes it a good choice for wick type hydroxyl systems. Perlite is also relatively inexpensive.

The biggest disadvantage of perlite is that it does not retain water, which means that it will be quickly watered between waterings. Perlite dust is harmful to health, so you should wear a dust mask when handling it.

Chapter 7: Mineral elements / nutrient mixing directions

Enhancement are the reason for every hydroponic system and since we have to meet all the needs of the plant in food, it is important to recognize what you are giving and what can be serious. With any improvement action plan, two factors you need to remember are right behind making your improvement - does it contain the set of parts needed to improve the plants in the right proportions. Also, with your fair and finished complementary action plan, what quality or `` CE '' should you achieve for your performance, timing and type of hydroponic structure and how would we measure it?

Way to improve

Different manufacturers like to buy a "mixed" supplement to an action plan that should basically be weakened (for fluid you think) or separated in water before use. Most of the time these `assembly accessories` come in 2, 3, 4 or even more` `parts '' so that the manufacturer can modify the range of mineral segments to take account of vegetation progress. either fruitful or for different crops. Surprisingly different brands of these mixed enhancements are available, in each case, different growers have overcome significant problems by trying to use the `house-drying` segment or different planned improvements. For plants that create in soil or ready-mix. Regularly, this kind of thing is not suitable for hydroponics, as they are not expected to be a "complete plant bed". It is always attractive to buy a development blend that is marketed specifically for "hydroponic" use and is "finished" with a plant base. To do this, hydroponic enhancement must have major segments for plant advancement:

- Nitrogen (N);
- Potassium (K);
- Phosphorus (P);
- Calcium (Ca);
- Magnesium (Mg);
- Sulphur (S);
- Iron (Fe);
- Manganese (Mn);
- Copper (Cu);
- Zinc (Zn);
- Molybdate (Mo);
- Boron (B);
- Chlorine (Cl)

The levels at which these parts are available in your hydroponic supplement generally vary between brands, as there is no single recommendation for obsessions. Various improvements may also include some of the "accommodation segments", for example nickel (Ni), cobalt (Co), silicon (Si) or selenium (Se). Although they are not "essential" (plants will currently produce without them), they can be useful for different yields.

Additional problems

Whether you develop your own improvement game plan from the undoubted fertilizer salts or buy an already prepared brand, the problems can recur due to problems with one of the most important measures of the parts 'improvement. The common goals behind this are (1) the quality of the improvements may be too low, producing inappropriate improvements for factories in general. (2) The improvement formula you use may not be completely balanced and (at least one of the parts) may be inadequate. (3) Sometimes growers may inadvertently neglect one of the fertilizer salts or use discrete feces when the improvement formula has been measured. In addition, just to understand things, whether your answer is the same or not, the habitual and internal conditions of the plant interfere from time to time with the taking of explicit improvements and signs of deficiency.

Real estate signs

All the mineral parts the plant needs have their own "signs and defects" course of action and growers can understand how to spot their critical number. Countless signs are practically identical in appearance, others are incredibly obvious anyway, and the most unusual hydroponic books and cultures will explain in detail what these signs are. Briefly, the following symptoms have been reported below for all parts (which may vary between different plant types and depending on the source of the deficiency).

Symptoms of misuse

Nitrogen (N): The plants are short, the leaves will generally be a light green yellow when they hide, especially on the decanted leaves. On tomato plants, the underside of leaves and stems may develop a purple hue.

Phosphorus (P): Plants are normally disturbed and dark green in color. The signs first appear on the prepared leaves and plant improvement is constantly delayed. The lack of phosphorus in some plant species can be a direct result of the conditions that make it cold to recover this part, rather than the lack of phosphorus in the game improvement plan.

Potassium (K): The more sandy habitable leaves turn yellow with scattered spots, dark or dark, due to tissue death. An extraordinary deficiency will slow the plant and all the leaves will turn yellow and fold. On the salad leaf, the leaves can take on a yellowish and bronze appearance, starting with more prepared leaves.

Sulfur: There cannot be any sulfur deficiency - yellowing of the leaves may occur, which was first noticed on the new improvement.

Magnesium: deficiency is common on tomato crops, with more leaves in preparation, which leave the yellow parts between the green veins.

Calcium: young leaves are affected before they are more and more inhabited and become damaged, small with speckled or necrotic (dead) areas. The improved buds are destroyed and the ends of the roots can remove the pool. The cost of lettuce to salad is a reaction to the need for calcium, and yet it is reached across various segments that are unrelated to the lack of response. The decomposition of tomatoes with tomatoes is also obtained by the lack of calcium in the tissues of the natural product (exaggerated continuous improvements), and even more the problem of the transport of calcium in the plant under certain normal conditions.

Iron: The deficiency turns into a yellow-yellow color between the veins of the leaves which remain green, new progress and ever growing leaves (this is recalled by the lack of magnesium, which first appears on the more ready leaves) . On yields, for example for tomatoes, an iron deficiency can be demonstrated when the conditions are cold and not caused by a deficiency certified in the game plan.

Chlorine: the insufficiency is in the form of wrinkled leaves which then become yellow and necrotic, while the long bar turns into a bronze mask.

The quality of the game plan - underuse and overuse, evaluation As the improvement you use is made and balanced, the concentration or nature of the action plan will affect the improvement and progression of the plant. This is an explanation where it is essential to have an alternative to checking the flow of action centers, using an important unit of measurement. Currently, different manufacturers will operate in ppm, using TDS counters, in any case, the industry will now launch a systematization of the evaluation of units according to EC (electrical conductivity), which is an inappropriate and valid way to respond to your improvement screen. Everything that makes a TDS or ppm counter is really used to measure the EC action flow, up to that point, using the induced change to change it to PPM. The problem evolves is that this change of change is final from time to time, because different improvement plans with different syntheses of supplement segments will have different PPM values, so the use of a single change in value may be unthinkable outside. from the base. What the plant root system really responds to is osmotic amplification (or shrinking), so this is what we need to measure. There are different specific EC meters (sometimes called CF), and manufacturers generally use "water safe" pens. Depending on where you are on the planet, the units shipped to your meter can be unprecedented, in any case, it is certainly not difficult to switch between different EC units.

The most used units are the microsiemens / cm (EC) or the conductivity factor (CF) (depending on the country you are in). The different units used or relayed several times in the culture recommendations are: Millimhos, micromhos or millisiemens (mS). The change between these units is:

1 millisiemen (EC) goes up to 1 millimhos, approaches 1000 microsimens, goes up to 1000 millimhos, goes up to 10 CF.

Just move the decimal to switch between different units.

It should be noted that the correct EC boot for your particular performance and system. Several crops, for example, green lettuce and various green vegetables, tend to be much lower in EC than fruit yields, such as tomatoes, and each yield has its ideal EC motivation to progress perfectly. At a time when for a particular plant the EC is increasing at a high level, it will prove to be obvious indicators of yield. At high EC, plants experience "stress" when plant cells begin to lose water, switching to a more thoughtful mode of action involving the roots. Consequently, the basic sign of a supplement of "misuse" is to contract the factory, in any case, when a game plan sufficient for improvement is obtained. If the high EC conditions are not intense, the plants will adapt to these conditions and you will see an improvement which is "hard" in appearance - mostly dark green, then mostly, with shorter plants and more leaves. small. As the EC drops to fall, it recedes - more visible proportions of water are taken, the improvement will be brittle and discontinuous, and there will usually be a lighter green.

Chapter 8: Advanced nutrient management

For an experienced hydroponic grower, nutrient management is an opportunity to stimulate plant growth. For newcomers, this is a challenge. The difference is in knowledge, understanding and equipment. Consider the following questions to test your nutritional IQ.

What is the temperature of your nutrient solution, what is the range during the day and during the season?

How much "dissolved solids" is in the water you use to mix the nutrients, and does that vary by season? Does your water supplier give you good water from one tank at one time of the year and bad water from another tank in another?

Are there components in your water that could affect the availability of nutrients in your crop?

What is the "EC" or strength of your nutrient? Do you mix special mixtures of nutrients for different types of plants and for each stage of the crop life cycle?

Is your nutrient ph within a reasonable range?

Are there pathogens in your nutrient from contaminated water or diseased plants that could spread the disease to the rest of your crop?

Do you change your nutrients often enough to avoid excessive buildup due to salt buildup or a deficiency due to nutrient depletion?

Did you know that an important reason to change your dietary solution is to eliminate the waste that your plants reject in nutrients? Did you know that during the transition of plants, moisture and nutrients fall into your tank and nutrients can reach dangerous levels?

These are just a few basic questions that can help you better understand what you already know and what you may need to learn to get bumper crops every time. This discussion is specifically for the advanced grower who wants to get the best yield and is serious about being at the forefront of plant breeding technology. Amateur breeders don't usually have to worry about all of these issues, but keep reading right away. When problems arise and the crop does not grow as it should. The problem can often be attributed to nutrient management. Once you know what can go wrong, it is easier to identify the problem when it occurs.

The root environment is what separates hydroponics from tillage. In the soil, plants wait for rain or irrigation and their roots look for essential nutrients. With good and fertile soil and abundant aquatic plants thrive.

Advanced nutrient management for hydroponic producers Check nutrient IQ

In hydroponics, the roots of the plants we constantly supply with water, oxygen and nutrients - not looking for available nutrients or waiting for the next rain. The challenge for the producer is to be in tune with the needs of the plants and to avoid damaging the plants with an excess or deficiency of minerals, extreme pH and temperature values or a lack of oxygen. A few simple tools and techniques can make the difference between success and failure.

What is in your water?

The first question to consider is the quality of the water. With good fresh water, it is easy to succeed. Just add the right combinations of nutrients to the water and you're off and growing. If you have very hard water or water contaminated with sodium, sulfide or a number of heavy metals, you may need to filter the water using "reverse osmosis".

So what's in your water anyway? The most complete answer comes from the laboratory's analysis of water. If you are in the city's water system, call your water district and request a copy of their latest analysis.

Another approach - highly recommended - is to regularly check the water with a dissolved solids meter, also called an electrical conductivity meter (EQ) or parts per million (PPM). These instruments are one of the most important tools that a farmer will have and will use regularly.

All of these instruments work essentially the same way. They measure the electrical conductivity of water. The salts dissolved in most water allow it to conduct electricity. Pure water is a bad conductor because there are no conductive salts in impure water. Purified water will show little or no salt (conductivity) when tested with one meter of dissolved solids.

It is not uncommon to find high levels of salt in the water supply or municipal water supply. Calcium and magnesium carbonates are among the most common ingredients in well and well water. In fact, "water hardness" is defined as a measure of the content of calcium and magnesium carbonates or sulfates in the water.

Because calcium and magnesium are important nutrients for plants. water with a reasonable level of these elements can be good for hydroponics. However, even a good thing can become a problem if the levels are too high.

Typically, a calcium content greater than 200 PPM or 75 PPM for magnesium is at the threshold of over-the-counter hydroponic applications. Excess can cause other important elements of the nutrient solution to "lock in" and become inaccessible. For example. excess calcium can be combined with phosphorus to form calcium phosphate, which is not very soluble and is therefore not available for cultivation. The key is to start with decent water and add the right combination of nutrients.

Too hot, too cold

Another important factor is the water temperature. If your solution is too cold, the seeds will not germinate, the cuttings will not take root, and the plants will grow slowly - or stop growing and die. If it is too hot, the same seeds will not germinate, the cuttings will not take root and the plants will die from lack of oxygen or simply from heat stress. Most plants prefer a root temperature range between 65 degrees (18 C) and 80 degrees (27 C), colder for winter crops, warmer for tropical crops. When adding water to

Advanced nutrient management for hydroponic producers Check your IQ nutrient at the same temperature as the water in the tank.

Plants don't like rapid changes in temperature, especially in the root zone!

PH of water

A subject often discussed but rarely understood by many producers is the pH of nutrients. In general, we are concerned about pH and its effect on the availability of nutrients. For example, if the pH is too high, iron can become inaccessible. Although your nutrient solution may have an ideal iron content, your plants may not be able to absorb it, resulting in iron deficiency: the leaves of the plant turn yellow and weaken.

On the other hand, advanced hydroponic plant foods contain special "chelates" which are designed to ensure that iron is available in larger pH ranges. The result is that your crop will grow quite well. even at higher pH levels. However, high pH can otherwise damage plants. The cause of the high pH of the solution can be quite complex. Most of the city's water supply contains calcium carbonate to raise the pH of the water and prevent corrosion. Therefore, you start with water with an abnormal pH, usually 8.0 for city water.

The first way to get rid of it is to mix the fresh nutrient with water, let it stabilize for a while, and then test and adjust the pH. For city water supply, you will often need to add a little pH (usually phosphoric acid) to lower the pH of most plants, from 5.8 to 6.2.

As the plants grow. it is a good idea to periodically test the pH and adjust it if necessary. You can safely drop the pH between 5.5 and 7.0 without adjustment. in fact, constantly throwing chemicals into your system to maintain a perfect pH of 5.8 to 6.0 can do a lot of damage. It is common for the pH to rise for a while, and then again and again. This change indicates that your plants are absorbing nutrients properly. Adjust the pH only if it goes too far.

A pH below 5.5 or above 7.0 can mean problems. but don't overreact. An apparently sudden and dramatic change in pH can result from a faulty pH meter. If in doubt, recheck with the pH reagent kit (color matching) before adjusting the solution. Remember that all pH measurement methods are temperature dependent.

Media culpa

Another cause of unstable pH is poor quality culture. Stone wool and industrial grade gravel are known to have very high pH levels that raise the pH of your nutrients, often increasing constantly, often to dangerous levels.

An easy way to test a new culture medium is to put a portion of the medium - rock wool, gravel, soil - in a clean beaker and then immerse (soak) the sample. in distilled or "deionized" (chemically pure) water. Let it stand for a while, then test the pH of the water, record the pH, and continue to release the sample. From time to time test the pH for about a week until it stabilizes.

Did the pH drop to 8.0, maybe 9.0? The gravel of a building block can be up to 10.0 - torture root. dead with plants!

Advanced Nutrient Management for Hydroponic Manufacturers Check the IQ of the Nutrients

Never underestimate growing media as a source of pH problems. This is one of the main reasons why hydroponic "aquaculture" methods are gaining popularity compared to media-based hydroponics. The less media you use, the less trouble you have with pH instability and salt buildup. In addition, water culture systems require less water and nutrients than media-based methods, for greater efficiency and reduced evaporation.

Time for a change?

How often do you need to change your nutrient solution? It is one of the most frequently asked questions and one of the most difficult to answer. Many have tried to find a simple and easy to follow rule - once a week, every two weeks - but everyone is wrong! They are wrong because there is no easy answer. It all depends on the type, number and size of your plants. the capacity of the tank, the type and quality of nutrients you use, the quality of the water, environmental conditions such as temperature and humidity, and the type of hydroponic system used. Instead of a simple answer, we need a procedure that takes into account many of these variables and is sensitive to changing conditions.

It sounds complicated, but it's actually quite simple. All it takes is a little monitoring and basic record keeping. Start with a new nutrient tank and record the date, pH and EC or PPM of the solution. When you start the system, the level drops in the tank. Note the EC / PPM level and then fill the tank with fresh water. Check the nutrient concentration again. If nutrient strength has dropped significantly, add some nutrients to bring it back to specifications.

Make sure you record the amount of water you have added to fill the tank. Repeat the process each time you fill the system, carefully recording the amount of water added. When the total amount of water is added to the volume of your tank. it is time to empty and replace all the nutrient solutions.

For example, imagine a hydroponic system in a cold greenhouse in the spring with 24 strawberry plants and 20 gallon nutrients. Typically, such a system would require about 5 liters of water added each week. After four weeks, the plants will receive 20 liters - tank capacity. In this example, you must completely dry and replace the nutrients every four weeks.

Nutritious pathogens

The problem of the pathogen or disease in the nutrient solution can be serious. It is not uncommon for this to be a regional and seasonal problem. In the Netherlands, for example, fungi thrive in cold, humid environments during winter: the air is full of spores. In the Dutch winter, all types of soil-borne diseases become endemic and producers find it difficult to avoid infection. One of the reasons why Dutch producers so easily adopted hydroponics was to avoid diseases introduced into the country.

Keep your growing area clean. Never let the soil enter the nutrient flow. If the soil is accidentally inserted into the tank, the entire crop may be at risk. Some producers will place a foam pad soaked in disinfectant on the greenhouse door. All those entering must clean their shoes on this carpet before entering. It is an effective and practical way of preventing organisms from entering the greenhouse and endangering crops.

If an infected plant is introduced into the hydroponic system, the disease can spread throughout the crop. By the time the problem is noticed, it may be out of control. Plant diseases are beyond the scope of this article, but the best advice is to avoid the problem of working clean, planting only healthy, disease-free plants with care Advanced nutrient management for growers hydroponics Check the nutritional control of your IQ on the crop.

If you see records of diseases in a plant, delete them and destroy them quickly before the disease spreads. Carefully monitor the crop and destroy any plants showing signs of disease. It is better to lose a few sick plants than to risk the whole harvest.

If you are having a problem with the disease, it is a good idea to dry it completely and restore the nutrients after removing the diseased plants. If possible, there is nothing better than flushing the system by missing a day of nutrient-free fresh water. Then drain it and fill it with fresh nutrients. Rinsing between three or four nutrient changes can help maintain the purity of the root zone and the hydroponic system. Periodic flushing is particularly useful for gravel systems to eliminate the accumulation of salt in the medium.

To the extreme

For some amateur growers, especially those who come to hydroponics from the U-plant-em-and-mole gardening school, the techniques described above may seem too difficult and too long. Remember that hydroponics provides excellent control over the health and quality of plants grown today with the interest and skills to perform this control. This is the purpose of this article: to push it to the limit. Keep in mind that it is also possible to create a hydroponic garden that will surpass any garden garden by simply following the production instructions on system functioning and nutrient changes and paying attention to the condition of your plants. But even the most represented breeder can benefit from understanding a few basic concepts.

Water quality is a big advantage, bad water is a challenge. Use only the highest quality plant foods, specially designed for hydroponics. Low-quality plant foods and common fertilizers provide plants with poor and incomplete nutrition, cause the pH to drop, and sometimes contain impurities that can become toxic to hydroponic plants. Only high-quality plant foods can grow superior plants. Healthy plants grow faster, give higher yields and are resistant to disease and insects. Always weigh carefully when mixing fresh nutrients.

Keep notes of your observations of EC flow rates, pH values, total water consumption, temperature range, and comments on crop health and progress. Keep an eye on the pH and pay particular attention to the strength of the nutrients (PPM. EC, dissolved solids). Watch for disease and immediately remove and destroy diseased plants.

Control nutrient temperature - Use high quality aquarium heaters to heat nutrients in winter, look for "coolers" to cool nutrients in summer if high nutrient temperatures become an issue. People in aquaculture or fish farming have developed excellent coolers.

Super nutrients

Super Veg An and B - All the underlying segments (micro) are joined for a rich vegetative progression. Super Veg An and B has an adjusted pH to reach 6.0 to 6.5, zero high / low pH is required for all purposes. As you mention, search for both An and B.

Super Bloom An and B - Provides a minimal source of supplementation, just like the right elements (microphones) follow to grow huge various germs. balanced pH, will not waste plants and will essentially collect yields. As you mention, search for both An and B.

A prominent blend when added to most game improvement plans. Dutch scientists, after evaluating tests and research, have separated and refined a protein that improves rapid division of plant cells and prolongs the thickness of cell division. Although different improvements have resulted in different cases of increased yields and flavor improvements, the B-CUZZ continues!

- Completely regular
- Fully ideal for hydroponic applications
- A descriptive gift with a course included in each request.

Dynagro is a one-way formula that contains a huge range, a smaller range and the parts that follow.

Create - Grow is a combination designed for artistic vegetative improvement

Hydroponics in general, Flora's action plan is an addition to the three-zone formula. Each of the three species is mixed differently depending on the stages of collecting and improving the plants. The plans are on the bottle. General hydroponics proposed in step 3-2-1 for an intensive progression of the plant. At the vegetative stage, a mixture of 3 teaspoons of Grow, 2 teaspoons of Micro, 1 teaspoon of Bloom for each liter of water and at the flowering stage is recommended, 3 teaspoons of Bloom, 2 spoons teaspoon of Micro and 1 teaspoon of Grow per liter of water.

Mixture of hydroponic systems

Feed the soil.

The best strategy for mixing nutrient solutions.

Mixing up a game plan for improvement can be as simple as applying a bottle of pus. Most of the recommended fertilizer rates generally provide a reasonable stock of the improvements that the plants need.

Nevertheless, some are absolutely better than others and are progressively unambiguous with the needs of specific plants. The brands, for example, Greenfire® Earth Juice, Welcome Harvest Farmtm, General Hydroponics®, Advance Nutrients®, Supernatural® and others, provide the conditions for creation in soil structures, without soil or hydroponic structures.

Preparation, on the other hand, can turn into science depending on what the practitioner seeks to accomplish. Several product manufacturers manage all parts by adapting their conditions to explicitly meet needs throughout all periods of progression.

Choosing to cope with the prerequisites of a particular strain is another important factor in creating an appropriate agreement that addresses the condition in order for the manufacturer to be able to provide perfect food and additional costs.

It is possible to select parts per million (PPM) of a particular segment, for example nitrogen from the steps of the segments recorded on the excretory pack.

Detection of parts per million

The plan for enhanced complex treated games should be 1,000 to 1,500PM for safe gaming when in doubt, but custom modifications (such as 800PPM) may be made depending on the factory.

The TDS counter will give the PPM test (parts per million). Excessive counters measure the volume of rooms and can be used to manage all costs with the bases without a doubt, since unambiguous improvements can be incorporated when factories use explicit improvements.

The characteristic or fabricated plan of games regularly treated for improvement must not exceed 1500 pPM. With a usual characteristic or inventive course of action, the grower can take into account a measurement of explicit segments, in the way that many excretions do not contain salts of square progression when they have an abundant response. For example, when Earth Juice® Grow and Earth Juice® Bloom are used to obtain perfect nitrogen and calcium PPM, the PPM on the meter would be lower than if the response to calcium nitrate was used to obtain proportional nitrogen and PPM calcium.

Checking a hydroponic/aeroponic reservoir

Energetic Plants.

Energetic plants will when all is said in done use more water than supplement. Right now, the underlying 2 to about a month, adding plain water to an archive is in all likelihood all that is required, in light of the fact that game plan will get saline (for instance 1,800PPM) when a plant takes in water missing a ton of supplement.

Until plants start to use a decent proportion of supplement, it can't to do complete store changes considering the way that there are supplements that have not been used by the plants. All things considered,

600 to 1,000PPM is good for seedlings and vegetative advancement.

Developing plants

It doesn't harm to make an answer on the frail side (for instance 1,000PPM) until plants start to use an equalization of supplement and water, in light of the fact that PPM will climb as water is used by the plants.

Right when plants use equal measures of supplement and water, adding 1,000 to 1,500PPM concentrated course of action is recommended.

Right when plants use more enhancement than water, including a concentrated course of action about 1,500PPM is proposed, with the exception of if a more grounded obsession is required to keep PPM at perfect levels. One should endeavor to keep the PPM near 1,500PPM in the store when liquid is incorporated. Thusly, the game plan will stay inside the 1,000 as far as possible, even as PPM progressively drops as plants use more enhancement than water.

Exactly when a store needs developing (for instance every 1 to around fourteen days), it is a shrewd idea to allow the response for miss the mark. For example, if a full store is at 1,500PPM, it is possible to allow water and supplement to lower to a level, for instance, 800PPM. This will give to some degree flush since the course of action is a little on the fragile side. Additionally, by and by there is simply to some degree liquid to guide out of the store before another course of action is incorporated, right now support.

A main issue huge is that greater stores will have less changes in PPM and pH and will hold support down.

Two gallons of course of action for each plant in a top-dealing with structure is a respectable indicate place in a store. This size compensates only for minor step by step instabilities in PPM and pH.

Plants that are close to genuine light will experience supplement more quickly than plants that get less outstanding light.

Exactly when plants don't get the correct bits of sustenance, supplement insufficiencies occur. Right when a need occurs, plants ordinarily change concealing from green to green-yellow to yellow. Insufficiencies are every now and again a sign that the archive needs a change, or express segments ought to be added to the inventory.

Exactly when a deficiency occurs, it is recommended to give the plants the sustenance they long (for instance nitrogen or calcium). Nitrogen is the most notable insufficiency.

Needs should change inside a day or two after the right excrement is applied, and plants should come back to a strong green, aside from if the deficiency caused certified damage.

Step by step guidelines for the use and cleaning of tds counters

A. Younger anodes should be washed with clean or refined water or isopropyl alcohol and water. The Q tip helps clean terminals without waste.

The direct counter must be immersed in the adaptive game plan (i.e. 1000 PPM). A small support or shielding tip around the terminal fills up as a place where the course of action can change.

C. The dial should rotate until the test displays a game plan (for example, 1000 PPM).

D. The anodes should be cleaned again with bright or refined water.

E. The meter must be submerged in the store after incorporating the fertilizer.

F. A fertilizer (fertilizer) or water must be added to change the test between 1,000 and 1,500 per minute.

In the event that the PPM is higher than necessary, including water can weaken the response for a perfect PPM to develop. The meter is extremely futile in choosing the actual proportions of a characteristic or regularly produced course of action, and yet it is an average reference meter. Currently, there are sections of intricacies and planes characteristic of the invention, and the area advises the most ideal approach to achieve the perfect PPM of a particular segment (for example, nitrogen) in fertilizer to pages 88 to 90.

In a perfect world, a water source is close to 0 ppm, so water cannot have unwanted PPM which can set restrictions on the proportion of fertilizer added in response. There are a variety of decently sensitive machines, for example, welding machines and purifiers that displace annoying solids from the water supply.

Note: PPM readings may need to be used as a source of view when editing game plans, as they do not see verifiable parts per million responses. It is best to record parts per million of a manure or a particular segment with a few mathematical and scientific figures, as shown on pages 88 to 90.

Most meters are valued at less than $ 100. They measure PPM at size 100 (for example 100, 500, 1000, 1100). For a considerable number of individuals, these counters do this. Nevertheless, there are expensive counters that measure the response in a large collection of coins. These devices are intended for aquaculturists.

Selection of ppm without counter

Phase 1

The degree of segments in the manure (eg 20-20-20) is necessary to select the PPM.

The fertilizer packages are registered as NPK. N is all nitrogen and phosphorus is recorded as compound (P2O5) and potassium is recorded as (K2O).

Phosphorus (P) destroys 44% phosphorus (P2O5), potassium (K) 83% potassium (K2O).

To extract the PPM from manure 15-30-15, the basic progression is to take the three numbers and move the decimal point to the other side. According to nitrogen, the number would be 200. This number will give parts per million of nitrogen when a gram is added to each defect or liter.

For phosphorus, the manufacturer should increase by 300 by 0.44. For example, 300 x 0.44 = 132 pPM. This number will give parts per million of phosphorus when a gram is added to each square or liter.

For potassium, the manufacturer should build 150 to 0.83. For example, 150 x 0.83 = 124.5 PPM. This number will give parts per million of potassium when a gram is added to each quarter or liter.

Additional Note: Some growers prepare their plant foods with 5 to 7 base salts, as shown on pages 95 to 96.

Few detailed guidelines for obtaining the degree of part (for example, K = potassium) in the compound (for example K2SO4).

Here are the methods by which the required parts per million sulfur (S) and potassium (K) in potassium sulfate (K2SO4) are obtained.

A. It is the usual table of segments to obtain the atomic quantities of each particle. For example, potassium has the atomic number 19, sulfur has the atomic number 16 and oxygen has the atomic number 8.

B. Until, in order to select the degree of each segment, all the segments must have their atomic number extended by the quantity of particles in the joint. Regarding K2SO4, the atomic number of potassium, which is 19, copies 2 with 38, because there are 2 particles of potassium. Because there is only one molecule of sulfur, 16 expands by 1, which gives 16. Oxygen has 4 particles in the compound, currently expanding from 4 to 32.

C. By the total number of atomic numbers, it expands by the quantity of particles, then the sum of the particles copied on their atomic charges is incorporated.

D. To get the degree of each segment, the proportion of particles is expanded by the segment's atomic number. For example, because of potassium, 2 x 19 = 38.

E. The proportion of particles expanded by the segment's atomic number is detached by the entire of the extensive number of segments copied by their atomic numbers. Because of potassium, the 38 (number of particles x atomic number) is isolated by 86 = .44.

F. The number copied by 100 gives the rate. For potassium, .44 x 100 = 44%.

Phase 2

Finally, the rate number should have the decimal spot moved more than one spot to the other side. By virtue of potassium, the number would be 440. This number will give the parts per million of a segment when 1 gram is added to each quart or liter. Because of potassium , 1 gram of potassium sulfate in a quart of liquid will give 440PPM of potassium. Using a huge part of a gram for every quart will give 220PPM of potassium and 95PPM of Sulfur.

Phase 3

The level of dissolvability (and perfection) in water will make the last say. For example, a couple of game plans and powders will thoroughly separate into usable particles, while others won't be dissolvable in water, subsequently the segments won't be expeditiously available to plants. For example, gypsum (CaSO4) can't dissolvable in water, which makes it for all intents and purposes useless for hydroponic use. Regardless, gypsum separates step by step in soil where it works fine. All plans right now about 100% dissolvable in water.

Step by step instructions to Ph a solution

PH is the proportion of the hydrogen particle fixation in an answer or other medium. There are more hydrogen particles in a corrosive arrangement than in an essential arrangement. On a scale, a pH of 7.0 is unbiased, under 7.0 is acidic, and over 7.0 is basic.

A plant's admission of specific components is extraordinarily influenced by pH. A pH of 5.5 to 6.5 is the standard for this natural hydroponic strategy. A pH of 6.0 to 6.5 functions admirably for vegetative development and early blooming, while a pH of 5.5 to 6.3 functions admirably during blossoming.

A. The pH of plain water ought to be checked before including the manures. That pH number ought to be recorded where it can undoubtedly be found. On the off chance that the water pH is the equivalent later on, it is simpler to make a snappy equation utilizing similar composts without estimating.

B. The entirety of the composts can be included and blended well. The amounts ought to be recorded for future reference.

C. A perfect pH pen ought to be adjusted at 7.0, which is the pH perusing of the aligning arrangement.

D. The pen ought to be plunged into the arrangement and pH up or pH down ought to be included until the perusing is in the favored 5.5 to 6.5 territory.

Instances of natural pH up are preparing pop (sodium bicarbonate), Earth Juice® Natural Up and wood cinders. There are unending pH up arrangements accessible anyplace garden supplies are accessible. Heating soft drink ought to be utilized cautiously, in light of the fact that a lot of sodium can't. Luckily, sodium can be flushed out with plain water.

The plants can retain ill-advised measures of sodium if the potassium levels are not adequate. Utilizing taking care of mixes that don't shake the pH level methods practically zero pH up is required.

A case of natural pH down is the expansion of Earth Juice® Natural Down, and Greenfire® Earth Juice Grow. White flour and vinegar have been accounted for to work fine. There are numerous brands of pH down accessible.

Recording the amount of pH up or pH down that is included (for future reference) is a decent strategy for assembling an indistinguishable arrangement later on.

E. The terminals ought to be flushed in clean water before the meter is killed.

Ph drift

The pH ought to be checked day by day and balanced if essential in light of the fact that many treated arrangements will float altogether upward or descending in pH in under 24 hours. Natural manures will in general float upward in pH after blended, and may keep on doing so a day or up to a couple of days after the arrangement is blended. Including molasses and staying away from specific manures can keep the upward pH float in an answer (natural or synthetic natural) to a base.

For compost arrangements with natural supplements, pH float is generally basic after the arrangement is blended, and when certain supplements in the store come up short.

Making a natural (or concoction natural) arrangement daily or two ahead of time, with molasses (1.5ml per gallon of water) is a decent beginning stage.

The most effective method to use and clean the Ph pen

In the event that a pH pen can't after every day it is utilized, it tends to be difficult to get exact readings and it may not align to the right perusing, particularly if natural composts are utilized. Utilizing a cleaning arrangement before it is taken care of aligns the pen precisely. The pen ought to be permitted to remain damp when it is taken care of. A couple of drops of aligning arrangement in the base top enables the terminals to remain soggy.

Cleaning the pH pen with clean faucet water and a Q-tip works as well, and sets aside cash. At the point when a Q-tip is utilized, it is prescribed to tenderly force the cushion away from the stick so the delicate cotton-batting can be moved between intense spaces. Care ought to consistently be taken with the glass, since it can break and begin to give abnormal readings without a cultivator seeing the mistake.

After the pen is flushed, pH cushion 7.0 arrangement is utilized to adjust the pen. The meter should peruse 7.0. It might take a few seconds to arrive at a steady perusing. The pen can peruse 7.2 for a couple of moments, and afterward it can gradually descend before it peruses a consistent 7.0.

A modest jug of pH 4.0 ought to be utilized now and again to decide the state of the pH meter so as to see that the pen aligns at two unique numbers, 4.0 and 7.0.

After the pH pen is adjusted, it ought to be washed well with clean water before taking a perusing. The pen ought to be washed well with clean water after each perusing. In the event that the water is acceptable, clean running virus faucet water, the pen will regularly remain at one number when it is washed.

In the event that the pH pen is truly perfect and aligned appropriately, it should remain adjusted for a few readings.

At the point when the adjustment does peruse another way it is most likely on the grounds that the pen needs a cleaning. On the off chance that the meter can't and it is adjusted, all readings can be incorrect. Frail batteries can likewise lose the readings and make the pH pen work at a more slow speed.

Picking a hydroponic medium

Picking the best possible hydroponic medium is the most significant factor for a fruitful hydroponic nursery. All mediums respond to a preparing program in an unexpected way, and the expense of mediums shifts drastically.

Some neighborhood materials (for example fir bark, wood chips, little stones, and coconut strands) are accessible locally at a modest cost. Most enormous scope hydroponic ranches utilize huge amounts of neighborhood materials to minimize the expenses, yet a specialist may improve yields from business items, for example, earth, rockwool, or sanitized soilless blend that is modest and helpful for littler nurseries.

For a specialist, buying a hydroponic medium (for example rockwool) from the neighborhood garden shop might be a less expensive (and better quality) arrangement than finding a free medium.

For any medium, it is sheltered to take care of for 3 to 6 days, at that point flush for 1 day with plain. A choice with flushing is to utilize plain water and 1 to 2ml of hydrogen peroxide to guard against bothers in the root zone. A producer can flush all through a vegetation's cycle, until collect is inside about fourteen days.

Two weeks preceding harvest, producers frequently flush out the medium with plain water, a clearing arrangement followed with plain water, or a low PPM arrangement (for example 0 to 400PPM) to get most extreme flavor.

Getting ready mediums

Perlite compacts and should remain in a compartment of water for about a half hour. Fine particles of perlite will sink to the base of the water. The coasting perlite is valuable. The worst of the worst can go into fertilizer or nursery. Perlite is a decent medium, yet it doesn't stick onto components. In this way, plants must be very much taken care of.

Mud glides, and ought to be drenched or showered until the water going through it turns out to be clear. Flushing mud is like washing rice until the water runs clear. Dirt is contrarily charged and draws in positive particles, for example, calcium and potassium.

Drenching rock-like mediums, for example, mud in water and 35% hydrogen peroxide (for example 2 to 5 ml for every gallon of water) assists with sanitizing the medium from any potential infections. Sun heat cleans mediums as well.

Cautious Alert: Perlite and different mediums can stop up the taking care of framework and keep the arrangement from siphoning in or depleting. All screens and channels may require an occasional cleaning and the siphon ought to have underwear hose (whenever utilized) cleaned during a store change.

Reusing mediums

All mediums (with the exception of expendable mediums like rockwool) can be reused if all roots are expelled from the medium, and medium is cleaned between crops. For instance, mud, soilless blend, and round stones can be utilized uncertainly. Mediums can securely be sanitized with an utilization of 35% hydrogen peroxide (around 5 ml for each gallon of water).

Most mediums, for example, perlite can be treated the soil or utilized promptly to improve soil. For instance, separated wood chips can go into fertilizer, while perlite and soilless blend can go legitimately into the nursery.

Mediums ought to be cleaned when a harvest is finished to maintain a strategic distance from molds. Forms frequently develop while a soggy medium (for example dirt) sits unused. In the event that fundamental, a citrus chemical can be utilized to clean medium with the goal that all molds and waxy development are expelled.

After the citrus chemical is applied, the medium ought to be flushed with plain water to expel the cleanser like air pockets. A little extra chemical in the medium won't hurt the plants.

Reusing soilless mix

At the point when the indoor or open air crop is done, soilless blend can be sanitized with calcium peroxide so the medium can be reused to develop more harvests. This is useful, in light of the fact that after each harvest is done, the develop blend holds its venture esteem, since it tends to be reused uncertainly.

Just new composts should be included for each extra yield. Compound manures can be applied somewhat heavier in regions of sufficient precipitation in light of the fact that the blend will get a characteristic flush.

Chapter 9: Mineral deficiencies in plants

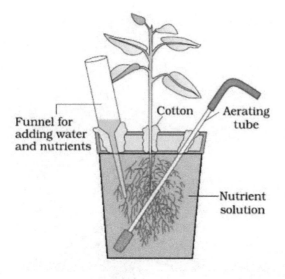

Funnel for adding water and nutrients

Cotton

Aerating tube

Nutrient solution

Ph acidbase

Chemical change leads to the production of new substances; these substances can be beneficial or harmful (and sometimes both!). Acids and bases are two types of substances that are very important in everyday life.

Acids are acidic, water soluble substances that are very useful in industry, household cleaning and cooking products; some examples are vinegar, vitamin C tablets, bicarbonate of soda, aspirin, lemon juice and cream. Vinegar is a solution of approximately one part acetic acid per 20 parts water - such a mixture of acid and water is called an acid solution. Lemons and grapefruits have a supple taste because they contain an acid called citric acid. Baking powder contains a dry acid called tartaric acid. Another very important acid is stomach acid (dilute hydrochloric acid) that helps digest our food. Acids that are not diluted in water are dangerous - they undergo chemical changes so easily that they can react with the skin and cause burns.

The bases are bitter, water soluble substances which are also very useful. Examples of basics are ammonia, bicarbonate of soda and a drain cleaner. The base is also used in some batteries. Water-forming solutions are called basic or alkaline solutions. The bases are also very reactive and have to be handled with extreme caution as they are easy to react with as well.

You've probably heard of antacids. These substances are safely swallowable bases that react with gastric acid. The chemical change in which an acid reacts with a base is called neutralization. This is called neutralization because equal amounts of acid and base create a solution that is neutral - neutral or basic acid. Antacids are used when the stomach contains too much acid, which irritates the gastric mucosa.

The pH scale is a measure of the acidity or base of a solution. This scale ranges from 0 for extremely acidic solution to 14 for extremely basic solution. The pH of the neutral solution is 7. The drop of one unit on this scale represents a tenfold increase in acidity. Most plants prefer a slightly acidic pH of 6.0 to 6.5. Appropriate pH values are important for the plant to absorb all the nutrients contained in the solution. One of the most common problems associated with home breeders is high or low pH. These problems manifest quickly and can be fought quickly and easily!

Most tap water has a slightly basic pH of 7 to 8, the nutrient that we mix in the solution is acid-based and adjusts the pH to one point or lower. However, we may need to adjust further by using a stable and usable acid such as dilute phosphoric acid. This is the most common scenario.

Maybe the source of water we use is acidic (for example, some well and groundwater) and after mixing the nutrients we need to adjust the pH higher. In this case, we would use a stable and usable alkali such as dilute di-potassium phosphate.

A simple method can be used to detect whether the solution is acidic or basic. An indicator is a substance that changes color depending on whether it is in acidic or basic solution. Electronic meters are also available to easily check the pH of the solution. They are simply immersed in the solution and deliver digital reading.

Perhaps one of the most important aspects of gardening, pH is very important in hydroponic and organic gardening as well as in regular "on the ground" gardening. The pH is measured on a scale of 1 to 14, 7 being "neutral". Acids are less than 7 and alkalis (bases) are more than 7.

This article discusses the pH of hydroponic gardening and the availability of nutrients at different pH levels in soil-free growth medium. Organic gardening and dirt have different levels, so the following table does not apply to them.

To be technical, the term pH refers to the potential content of hydrogen-hydroxyl ions in a solution. The solutions ionize into positive and negative ions. If the solution contains more hydrogen ions (positive) than hydroxyl ions (negative), it is acid (1-6.9 on the pH scale). Conversely, if the solution contains more hydroxyl ions than hydrogen, it is alkaline (or base), with a range of 7.1 to 14 on the pH scale.

The pH scale is logarithmic, which means that each change of unit is equivalent to a change of ten in the concentration of hydrogen / hydroxyl ions. In other words, a solution at pH 6.0 is 10 times more acidic than a solution at pH 7.0, and a solution at pH 5.0 would be 10 times more acidic than a solution at pH 6.0 and 100 times more acidic than a solution at pH 7.0. This means that when you adjust the pH of a nutrient solution and you have to move it 2 points (example: 7.5 to 5.5), you will have to use 10 times more adjustments than if you move the value of the pH only 1 point (7.5 to 6.5).

Why is ph important?

When the pH is not at the right level, the plant will lose the capacity to absorb some of the essential elements necessary for healthy growth. For all plants, there is a certain level of pH that will give optimal results (see Table 1 below). This pH level will vary from plant to plant, but generally most plants prefer a slightly acidic breeding environment (between 6.0 and 6.5), although most plants can still survive in an environment with a pH between 5.0 and 7.5.

When the pH exceeds 6.5, certain nutrients and micronutrients begin to precipitate out of the solution and may adhere to the walls of the reservoir and growth chambers. For example: iron will precipitate approximately at pH 7.3 and there is almost no iron in the solution at approximately 8.0. For your plants to use nutrients, they must be dissolved in solution. Once the nutrients are precipitated out of the solution, your plants can no longer absorb them and will suffer (or die). Some nutrients will precipitate out of the solution even when the pH drops.

Chapter 10: Ph acidbase

As a general rule, the pH meters should be adjusted from time to time, as the meters may float, and to ensure accuracy, you should check the alignment regularly. The tip must be placed in the anode storage or in the pillow position. The tip should never dry.

Because of the way pH meters have a separation rating without notice, it is a good idea to keep the crisis in a mood to check the pH (paper test strip or liquid test packaging test) by problem.

Change ph

There are several synthetic compounds used by a plant specialist in their spare time to change the pH. The best known are probably corrosive phosphorus (to lower the pH) and potassium hydroxide (to raise the pH). These two synthetic preparations are moderately protected, despite the fact that they can cause consumption and must never interact with the eyes. Most hydroponic supplies sell pH agents that are weakened to a level that is sensitive and easy to use. Concentrated agents can cause huge pH changes and change the pH disappointingly.

Several different synthetics can be used to modify the pH of hydroponic supplements. Nitrogen and corrosives with sulfur can be used to lower the pH, but they are much more dangerous than corrosion with phosphorus. The nutritious extract of citrus fruits is in some cases used in natural plantations to lower the pH.

Add supplements to the water continuously before checking and changing the pH of your supplement program. The fertilizer will generally lower the pH of the water due to the collection of the ingredients. After including extras and mixing arrangements, check the pH using whatever it implies. If the pH needs to be balanced, add the appropriate agent. Use modest amounts of pH agent until you are familiar with the process. Reconfirm the pH and readjust the above steps until the pH level is where you need to be.

The pH of the supplement program will increase as the plants use the food supplement. Thereafter, the pH should be periodically checked (and balanced if important). To start, I recommend that you constantly check your pH. Each image will change the pH at an alternative speed which will condition many elements.

Chapter 11: Foods grown in hydroponics

Hydroponics is a type of farming where plant roots develop, not in soil, however in supplement advanced water. It's an incredible technique for developing nourishment inside and in little spaces. With the expansion of programmed controls, it tends to be almost upkeep free.

Hydroponic historical roots

Hydroponic planting has establishes in old history, perhaps as far back as the principal century in antiquated Rome, when Emperor Tiberius needed cucumbers developed all year at his royal residence. In 600 B.C., plant specialists at the Hanging Gardens of Babylon – one of the seven miracles of the old world – may have utilized hydroponic standards. Further south, in the tenth and eleventh hundreds of years, the Aztecs built up an arrangement of hydroponic gliding gardens or chinampas. Incapable to develop crops on Lake Tenochtitlan's muddy shores, these early hydroponic ranchers constructed pontoons made of reeds, permitting the plant roots to slide through the structure's openings profound into the water.

When known as nutriculture and chemiculture, the term hydroponics gets its significance from the Greek words for water (hydro) and working (ponos) – working water. The term turned into a piece of the plant vocabulary when Dr. William F. Gericke of the University of California, Berkeley led investigates plant nourishment for enormous scope business cultivating applications. Outside the lab, Gericke got disliked with his neighbors when he grew 25-foot-high tomato vines in his lawn utilizing just mineral supplement arrangements.

How it works?

Plants developed hydroponically don't rely upon soil to acquire supplements. Rather, a pH-controlled supplement rich water gives what the plant needs to flourish by moving the nourishment straightforwardly to the plant roots, where it's quickly assimilated.

Hydroponics use shut circuit controlled frameworks which empower nursery workers to keep up ideal developing conditions. In an indoor framework, fake electric lights duplicate the sun's common light to empower photosynthesis. As plants require sufficient air course to get the carbon dioxide required for photosynthesis, indoor hydroponic frameworks normally incorporate fans or a venting framework.

No dirt methods no weeds, so plants developed hydroponically don't require any destructive herbicides. As soil regularly contains illnesses which can be transmitted to plants, hydroponic plants will in general be more infection and nuisance safe, in spite of the fact that not totally. As in soil-based developing, hydroponic plants can pull in bugs. Be that as it may, bugs will in general be negligible because of the controlled developing condition. Hydroponic plants are not really natural, yet cultivators can control bothers utilizing organic strategies in lieu of unsafe pesticides.

'Dry spell friendly' and water-conserving

Since water is provided through a recycling framework, hydroponics utilizes about 90% less water than conventional soil-based developing techniques, in this manner monitoring water – an invite idea during times of dry season.

Extraordinary for small-space living and indoor gardening

Hydroponic frameworks are ideal for nursery workers living in little spaces, as they require next to no area. In a similar measure of room, developing hydroponically delivers multiple times the measure of harvests of conventional soil-based systems. Most home frameworks are anything but difficult to set up, and moving the nursery is no laborious errand, as the frameworks are commonly easy to move.

Can be almost maintenance-free

Some hydroponic frameworks are about attachment and-play, as they highlight programmed controls which screen water and supplement levels, and a clock to oversee water system and include supplement arrangement when required.

Chapter 12: Postharvest handling systems

"Negligibly prepared" plant items are arranged and taken care of to keep up their crisp nature while giving accommodation to the client. Delivering insignificantly handled items includes cleaning, washing, cutting, coring, cutting, destroying, etc. Different terms used to allude to insignificantly handled items are "softly prepared," "incompletely prepared," "freshprocessed," and "preprepared."

Insignificantly prepared foods grown from the ground incorporate stripped and cut potatoes; destroyed lettuce and cabbage; washed and cut spinach; chilled peach, mango, melon, and other natural product cuts; vegetable bites, for example, carrot and celery sticks, and cauliflower and broccoli florets; bundled blended servings of mixed greens; cleaned and diced onions; stripped and cored pineapple; new sauces; stripped citrus organic products; and microwaveable crisp vegetable plate.

Though most nourishment preparing systems balance out the items and extend their capacity and timeframe of realistic usability, light handling of products of the soil expands their perishability. Along these lines and the requirement for expanded sanitation, arrangement and treatment of these items require information on nourishment science and innovation and postharvest physiology.

Development sought after has prompted expanded promoting of new agricultural items in delicately prepared structure. An industry devoted to this sort of nourishment preparing has been built up, and the

National Association of Fresh Produce Processors was as of late shaped.

Physiological responses

Negligible handling for the most part builds the paces of metabolic procedures that cause decay of new items. The physical harm or injuring brought about by planning builds breath and ethylene creation in practically no time, and related increments happen in paces of other biochemical responses liable for changes in shading (counting sautéing), flavor, surface, and nourishing quality, (for example, nutrient misfortune). The more noteworthy the level of preparing, the more prominent the injuring reaction. Control of the injury reaction is the way to giving a handled result of good quality. The effect of wounding and injuring can be diminished by cooling the item before preparing. Severe temperature control subsequent to handling is additionally basic in decreasing injury actuated metabolic movement, as appeared in the breath information of flawless and destroyed cabbage put away at various temperatures. Different systems that considerably lessen harm incorporate utilization of sharp blades, upkeep of stringent sterile conditions, and effective washing and drying (evacuation of surface dampness) of the cut item.

Microbiological concerns

Products of the soil are natural specialties for a differing and evolving microflora, which as a rule does exclude types pathogenic to people. Unblemished foods grown from the ground are sheltered to eat somewhat in light of the fact that the surface strip is a powerful physical and compound obstruction to most microorganisms.

What's more, if the strip is harmed, the corrosiveness of the mash forestalls the development of living beings, other than the acidtolerant parasites and microscopic organisms that are the deterioration creatures for the most part connected with rot. On vegetables, the microflora is overwhelmed by soil life forms. The typical decay verdure, including the microbes Erwinia and Pseudomonas, ordinarily have an upper hand over different creatures that might be destructive to people.

Changes in the ecological conditions encompassing an item can bring about huge changes in the microflora. The danger of pathogenic microbes may increment with film bundling (high relative dampness and low oxygen conditions), with bundling of results of low salt substance and high cell pH and with capacity of bundled items at too high temperatures (>5°C or 41°F). Nourishment pathogens, for example, Clostridium, Yersinia, and Listeria can possibly create on negligibly prepared foods grown from the ground under such conditions.

With insignificantly handled items, the expansion in cutdamaged surfaces and accessibility of cell supplements gives conditions that expansion the numbers and kinds of organisms that create. Besides the expanded treatment of the items gives more noteworthy chance to tainting by pathogenic creatures.

Microbial development on negligibly handled items is controlled chiefly by great sanitation and temperature the executives. Sanitation of all gear and utilization of chlorinated water are standard methodologies. Low temperature during and in the wake of handling for the most part impedes microbial development however may choose for psychrotropic life forms, for example, Pseudomonads. Dampness increments microbial development, in this way evacuation of wash and cleaning water by centrifugation or different techniques is basic. Low dampness diminishes bacterial development, in spite of the fact that it likewise prompts drying (shrinking and wilting) of the item. Low oxygen and raised carbon dioxide levels, regularly related to carbon monoxide, impede microbial development. Plastic film bundling materials alter the moistness and air organization encompassing handled items and hence may change the microbial profile.

Item preparation

Negligible preparing may happen in an "immediate chain" of readiness and dealing with in which the item is handled, dispersed, and afterward promoted or used. Numerous items are likewise taken care of in an "interfered with chain" in which the item might be put away previously or in the wake of preparing or might be handled to various degrees at various areas. In light of this variety in time and purpose of handling, it is helpful to have the option to assess the nature of the crude material and anticipate the timeframe of realistic usability of the prepared item.

Insignificantly handled items might be set up at the wellspring of creation or at local and nearby processors. Regardless of whether an item might be handled at source or locally relies upon the perishability of the

Postharvest handling systems

Handled structure comparative with the unblemished structure, and on the quality required for the assigned utilization of the item. Handling has moved from goal (nearby) to source processors as upgrades m gear, altered climate bundling, and temperature the board have opened up.

Previously, prepared lettuce activities frequently rescued lettuce staying in the fields in the wake of collecting for crisp market. It is currently perceived that first-cut lettuce ought to be utilized for most extreme handled item quality. Subsequent to cutting and coring, piece size might be diminished with turning blades or by attacking saladsize pieces. Harm to cells close to cut surfaces impacts the time span of usability and nature of the item. For instance. Destroyed lettuce cut by a sharp blade with a cutting movement has a capacity life around twice that of lettuce cut with a cleaving activity. Time span of usability of lettuce is less if a dull blade is utilized instead of a sharp blade.

Washing the cut item evacuates sugar and different supplements at the cut surfaces that favor microbial development and tissue staining. In view of contrasts in arrangement and arrival of supplements with preparing, a few items, for example, cabbage are known as "messy" items. It is alluring to keep up independent handling lines, or altogether clean the line before another item follows cabbage. Free dampness must be totally evacuated in the wake of washing. Centrifugation is commonly utilized, despite the fact that vibration screens and air impacts can likewise be utilized. The procedure should expel at any rate a similar measure of dampness that the item held during preparing. It has been indicated that expulsion of somewhat more dampness (i.e., slight parching of the item) favors longer postprocessing life.

Bundling, modified atmospheres, and handling

Polyvinylchloride (PVC), utilized basically for overwrapping, and polypropylene (PP) and polyethylene (PE), utilized for sacks, are the movies most broadly utilized for bundling negligibly handled items. Multilayered films, frequently with ethylene vinyl acetic acid derivation (EVA), can be made with contrasting gas transmission rates. For lettuce prepared at source, a 2.5 mil 8 percent EVA co-expelled PE sack has been utilized. Items are regularly bundled under halfway vacuum or subsequent to flushing with various blends of gases (oxygen, carbon dioxide, carbon monoxide, as well as nitrogen). Vacuum bundling and gas flushing set up the changed climate rapidly and increment the timeframe of realistic usability and nature of handled items. For instance, carmelizing of cut lettuce happens, before an advantageous environment is built up by the item's breath. For different items, for example, fastrespiring broccoli florets, impermeable hindrance films are utilized with penetrable layer "patches" to alter the environment through the item's breath. It isn't yet concurred what are the perfect movies and airs for negligibly handled items. Notwithstanding unique climate prerequisites for various items, the particulars of the dealing with chains must be considered, particularly their time postponements and temperature changes.

The altered climates that best keep up the quality and capacity life of insignificantly handled items have an oxygen scope of 2 to 8 percent and carbon dioxide groupings of 5 to 15 percent.

Carbon monoxide convergences of 5 to 10 percent under low oxygen (<5 percent) conditions impede carmelizing and diminish microbial development, protracting timeframe of realistic usability in lettuce and different items.

Chapter 13: Debate "organics" or "hydroponics"

There is a big public joke about compost assessment and "natural" techniques, many individuals may want to apply "organic" to hydroponics. Now, recognized segments of natural manure need living creatures in the dirt to transform "natural" materials into a structure usable by plants.

In hydroponics, we legitimately provide the minerals needed for plant development, completely eliminating the soil and soil requirement of creatures. The result is much higher development rates, yields and even better crop quality than natural techniques. This is not what few people need to hear, however, it is a simple logical truth - and for all intents and purposes, all horticulture and science researchers and instructors know this and will be the first to agree. In fact, the types of materials that are approved for use under the "natural" guidelines are not suitable enough to be used for hydroponics.

We use only the purest and pristine additives to mix our hydroponic fertilizers, including nutrients and pharmaceutical minerals. The "natural" guidelines do not allow the use of cleaned or refined fixings; all "natural" composts for fixing compost must be in their characteristic rough structure - the result may be an unfavorable degree of contaminants and poisons in addition to "extremely low insolvency." "Natural" means bureaucratic definitions, not science. Naturalness is the technique of cultivation, not the meaning of the product itself. There is nothing like "natural products", there are only "naturally developed products".

Given this trend, it is crucial to understand the reasons why "naturally" developed products increase this ubiquity. Customers must purchase products that are not damaged by dangerous synthetics or toxic substances. There is a growing interest in techniques sensitive to our fragile planet that do not harm dirt, water or the environment. Hydroponics strategies are a good fit for this quality arrangement when used appropriately. Hydroponics guarantees soil because it does not use soil. Less water is needed for hydroponics and therefore more food with less water can be grown. The manure we use for hydroponics is ultra pure and leaves no buildup in the hard surface. Because hydroponic innovations are more effective than soil strategies, more people with less region and natural impact can take care of them.

Organic hydroponic discussion

During the 1980s, Americans gradually became more aware of well-being. Cholesterol was off and practice became part of our daily schedule. Today, however, this remains constant, but much more. What we put in our bodies is scrutinized, even our food grown from the ground, which made it a natural modern expression of the 90s. People buy natural items for healthy skin. natural shampoos and even "natural clothing.

Everyone seems to need natural and hydroponic growers are very aware of this. Why are there hardly any established organic hydroponic producers in the United States at this time?

Many find it very difficult to develop their yields "naturally," but despite the fact that they follow most of the rules, they despise anything that cannot receive significant recognition or confirmation that they offer their products in most normal restaurants or food stores as "natural." Can it isolate it naturally from hydroponic techniques? Can not two advancers cooperate according to the affirmative guidelines of the current US states? ...

What's organic, what's not?

The Debate on various meanings of "natural," a considerable lot of which vary fundamentally. Each state has its own guidelines for naming produce as natural." Additionally, there are 36 non-legislative associations that can ensure" produce as natural. For instance, California cultivators who wish to sell their produce as "natural" must enlist with the California Department of Food and Agriculture and pass their review. be that as it may, California cultivators can likewise get confirmation through the California Certified Organic Farmers (CCOF), which really has better expectations for natural than the state has. The CCOF affirmation is discretionary, however, produce with California state enrollment and CCOF accreditation might be offered available to be purchased inside the state as "guaranteed natural" If the producer decides not to look for CCOF confirmation, the product can be offered available to be purchased in California as "natural," yet not "ensured natural. Any produce become outside of the United States can be sold as "confirmed natural" in the nation on the off chance that one of the 36 non-legislative associations affirms it.

Truth be told, produce from any state can be conceded accreditation from one of the non-administrative associations, regardless of whether it doesn't satisfy the natural guidelines for the state wherein it is being sold. Truly befuddling! What this all methods is that the "natural" name involves bureaucratic definitions which can differ from state to state and nation to nation. So as to bring a standard into play, the U.S. Division of Agriculture (USDA) - alongside state government controllers, non-legislative certifiers, buyers, industry intrigue gatherings, nourishment processors and different particular vested parties is composing a governmentally ordered arrangement of "natural" benchmarks.

No state will have the option to apply more stringent standards than those of the government. At some point this spring, the government measures will be discharged for a multi-day remark and survey period, and before the finish of 1996 or mid-1997, these models will become law, or "Frankenlaw;" we'll need to keep a watch out. The fundamental destinations of "organic" practice incorporate the accompanying:

- Avoidance of pesticides, by utilization of normal bug controls (additionally applied by numerous hydroponics producers);
- thinking about soil by recording supplements and treating the soil;
- control of supplement application with dependence on the cushion activity of humus got from fertilizer.

Soilless hydroponic development moderates supplement supply by the more precise estimations of the solvent supplement. Definitions blended to meet the ideal prerequisites of each plant species and development stage.

Numerous shoppers select "natural" produce, accepting this is the best way to be guaranteed of without pesticide nonhazardous nourishment. While "natural" cultivating strategies do deliver crops commonly better

84

than and more secure than those developed by agri-strategic approaches present-day hydroponic systems can advance similarly safe nourishment that by and large offers progress in sustenance and taste over their dirt developed "natural partners. In any case, to the customer, the mark checks, so an expanding number of cultivators all through the United States are attempting to get natural accreditation in any capacity whatsoever.

In the interim, this entire circumstance represents a tremendous difficulty to hydroponic cultivators who likewise need natural acknowledgment for their produce. The essential issue for natural hydroponic producers is in the plan of the soilless supplement arrangement. An optional issue, which concerns the government controllers, is standing out utilized hydroponic supplement and media, for example, Rockwool, are discarded. Since "natural" is to an enormous degree a cultivating theory on the side of a sound domain, the government concern is altogether sensible. Despite the fact that the last factor makes little difference to the quality and wellbeing of the product itself, the effect upon the planet is a genuine main impetus behind the issue of "natural" cultivating.

On the off chance that hydroponic cultivators can figure out how to totally reuse depleted water, supplements and media, at that point the contention for "natural hydroponic affirmation" turns out to be a lot more grounded, yet there's as yet the issue of detailing an acceptable natural hydroponic supplement blend. Natural supplement guidelines deny the utilization of numerous mineral salts and profoundly refined substances, including nourishment and pharmaceutical evaluation fixings that are critical for a fruitful hydroponic supplement plan.

Just foul minerals can be utilized on "natural" crops and these regularly don't break up well or contain amounts of contaminations, some of which are even moderately dangerous, however "normal and along these lines alright," as indicated by natural gauges, For instance, mined phosphate may contain over the top measures of fluoride, useful for teeth in extremely little amounts, yet unsafe to people in overabundance. Mined phosphate additionally can contain modest quantities of radioactive components, for example, radium, which discharges radon, likewise not useful for human wellbeing. Chlorides, as well, are allowed for natural development however they are normally mined, they can be terrible for the two plants and soil, particularly whenever utilized in overabundance.

A few soils utilized by natural ranchers contain\n such poisonous components as selenium, which can aggregate in the plant tissues and produce. Astounding, right? At the point when refined, any polluting influences or toxicities, for example, those recorded above are evacuated, yet refined minerals make for non-natural produce.

The Debate on microbial activity in the dirt and hence don't function admirably in hydroponic applications. There is likewise an issue that occasionally emerges when utilizing excrements. The Western Fertilizer Handbook, a significant guide for American ranchers, calls attention to that numerous gastrointestinal ailments can he followed back to excrements utilized on naturally outfit crops. In the late spring of 1995, a genuine episode of salmonella harming came about because of a natural melon crop developing in soil prepared with crisp chicken compost. The skins of the melons had gotten tainted and the microscopic organisms caused genuine intestinal disease for some shoppers.

Another point that can be made is that severe vegans or basic entitlements activists might be insulted by the utilization of blood, bone, horn, foot and quill dinners to develop their nourishment, however, these are essential supplements hotspots for natural ranchers. As should be obvious, this issue Is extremely intricate and there are numerous perspectives. Basically, however, "natural" cultivating is part theory and part procedure, yet shockingly characterized bureaucratically.

What's hydroponic, what's not?

On the off chance that a plant is developed without soil and with a total supplement arrangement that is hydroponics! It very well may be as straightforward as plants gleaming in sand, rock or Rockwool with a supplement dribble, or as unpredictable as a total water culture framework, for example, NFT (Nutrient Film Technique) or aeroponics. Regardless of what technique you use, the way to effective hydroponics is supplements. Hydroponic yields a circular segment raised on a culminated blend of essential, optional and smaller scale supplements. The equations for various harvests and conditions shift, yet all have been characterized by broad involvement in a wide assortment of yields developing in a wide range of situations all through the world. Issues may happen where water quality is poor and where ecological boundaries of high or low temperature and humidities place weight on crops; in any case, when a hydroponic office is appropriately arranged and introduced, the subsequent yields can be noteworthy. Information created in Europe, Israel, Canada, Australia, and the United States has characterized exact mixes of minerals for an assortment of harvests. The information is precise to the point that necessary components are indicated in mS (milisiemens) and uS (microsiemens), an arrangement of estimating by electrical conductivity and computing by nuclear weight. In light of these discoveries, the Dutch research station at Aalsmeer has sorted out supplement arrangements into three classes: "An" alludes to recipes that have been widely tried and can he thought about dependable. "B" connotes equations that are genuinely new yet working very well; a few changes can be required before moving up to a class "A." "C" recipes are trial; huge changes can be foreseen before moving up to class B or A. Recipes are characterized for a given yield developing under various conditions. For instance, components are indicated for the supplement repository, while a different detail is made for the supplements in the "root condition" if developing media is utilized, especially rockwool. The root condition for the most part has higher convergences of components since minerals will aggregate in rockwool. To test the fixation inside the media, the producer will crush some supplement out of an example of the media, do an essential conductivity and pH test, and now and again send the example to a lab for investigation. On the off chance that the convergence of components in the media transcends as far as possible, the cultivator should alter the plan of the supplement in the repository or run a flush through the media to bring down the supplement fixation inside the root zone. Another recipe might be characterized for non-recycling supplement, additionally called "race to-squander," where the supplement is sent from the repository on a single direction trip through rockwool onto the ground. This strategy is falling into disgrace because of the contamination brought about by the supplement run-off and disposed of rockwool.

Hydroponic produce and health

In 1994 a test was charged by a speculation gathering to decide the nutrient and mineral substance of hydroponically developed harvests in contrast with soil developed yields, both natural and nonorganic. Plant Research Technologies Laboratory in San Jose, California, broke down tomatoes and sweet peppers; those hydroponically developed utilized General Hydroponics' "Vegetation" supplements. The hydroponic produce indicated a noteworthy increment in nutrients and minerals advantageous to human wellbeing over the dirt developed produce. This information shows the significance of an adjusted supplement arrangement.

The harvests had been developed after the Dutch proposal for hydroponic tomatoes and sweet peppers, and not exclusively were they of higher healthy benefit, the flavor was answered to be remarkable. The hydroponic harvests were additionally broke down to look for synthetics on the EPA,s "need toxin list," of which, none were found. American agribusiness is starting to apply hydroponics on a critical scale.

Huge corporate offices are indicating benefits and producing high harvest yields with reliable quality at offices in Colorado, Utah, and Mexico. These establishments mark a significant point for hydroponic cultivating in the United Stares. On the off chance that the ventures demonstrate gainful over the long haul, at that point consistent development is going to proceed, gradually supplanting many field-developed yields in the commercial center. The British have been applying hydroponic cultivating to address customer issues for a considerable length of time. Cultivating cooperatives develop tomatoes, cucumbers and serving of mixed greens for an enormous scope.

Van Heinegen Bros. produces three pounds of hydroponically developed tomatoes every year for each man, lady, and kid in the British lsles. On the side of these ventures, the British government runs an examination office that researches improved hydroponic techniques, illness and vermin control and new plant assortments. The participation among government and ranchers has prompted improved harvest creation, quality and benefits. Albeit hydroponically developed produce, while normally liberated from pesticide and other concoction perils, doesn't commonly meet the somewhat limited meanings of "natural," it can offer predominant flavor, sustenance, appearance, freshness, and she1flife. Numerous little hydroponic cultivators are perceiving these market inclines and capitalizing on the colossal interest for better produce.

Little cultivators find that gourmet eateries and neighborhood markets are pleased to approach unrivaled quality produce, regardless of whether naturally or hydroponically developed. Since "natural" is practically impossible, an expanding number of hydroponic cultivators are advancing their produce as "sans pesticide." This gives the purchaser the consolation that their products of the soil have been developed after the most significant head of "naturally developed produce. One result of this division is that the expression "natural agribusiness" is declining for the expression "reasonable horticulture," which applies to both natural and hydroponic development. In spite of the fact that numerous natural cultivators look down on hydroponic innovation, the predominant quality and freshness of privately developed hydroponic produce is in actuality picking up advertise acknowledgment.

Another specialty is creating for little hydroponic producers, family cultivates, and even urban ranches in regions that have generally been served by huge corporate homesteads far away. The straightforward truth is that top quality naturally raised produce must have become under genuinely perfect conditions and just regularly in many pieces of the United States. This outcome in produce that is costly and recurrence inaccessible or sent from a remote place, making quality endure. In the "natural model, great soil is enhanced with fertilizer, blood feast, bone dinner, composts and a large group of other normal revisions.

These parts separate gradually in the dirt at a rate incongruity with the plants' development; a microbiological procedure is required to make the supplements accessible to the plants. These microorganisms incorporate numerous living beings that are all in a harmonious grasp with nature and the plants. At the point when done dexterously in the correct condition with the correct harvest, this is nature and cultivating at its best. In any case, it contrasts forcefully from the hydroponic model, where microorganisms are pointless for the plants to retain the readied supplements.

The supplement ingestion pace of a hydroponically developed plant is commonly a lot quicker than that of dirt developed plant since in hydroponics, supplements are in a flash solvent and accessible, as is fundamental oxygen. Hydroponic plants are typically developed in a generally sterile condition, and frequently with exact controls, from fake lighting to stretch out developing seasons to colorful PC frameworks that empower the producer to really tailor the earth to the yield wherein hydroponics turns out to be only one piece of the whole framework. Right now arrangement, work is diminished, yet plant development rates, yields and quality increment.

Numerous endeavors have been made to make the ideal natural hydroponic supplement, however, so far nothing matches the cleansed mineral salts utilized in planning hydroponic supplement arrangements. We note that the European Economic Community (EEC) has set up the class of "mineral natural" for nourishments developed with the necessary mineral supplements to enhance a natural base of nitrogen.

We recently addressed the way that United States rural guidelines are right now set and applied at the state level yet basically all states disallow the utilization of refined fixings to develop natural" crops; just mined minerals can be utilized. Shockingly, this blocks natural cultivators from utilizing pharmaceutical or nourishment grade fixings to detail manures. This could be a danger, however, in any event, mined minerals will separate in the dirt. Hydroponic cultivators, then again, must utilize refined minerals in light of the fact that mined minerals break up ineffectively in arrangements. As a result, it isn't at present down to earth to detail a top-qual.

Chapter 14: Beginner's growing tips

This page has been intended to help answer the significant inquiries starting producers may have when simply beginning in hydroponics. A great deal of these ideas are associated with one another. Follow the connections and put the bits of this developing riddle together.

The more you know, the simpler it is to develop!

Carbon dioxide

During photosynthesis, plants use carbon dioxide (CO_2), light, and hydrogen (generally water) to create starches, which is a wellspring of nourishment. Oxygen is emitted right now a result. Light is a key variable in photosynthesis.

Conductivity

Estimating supplement arrangement quality is a moderately straightforward procedure. Nonetheless, the electronic gadgets produced to accomplish this errand are very advanced and utilize the most recent chip innovation. To see how these gadgets work, you need to realize that unadulterated water doesn't direct power. Be that as it may, as salts are broken up into the unadulterated water, power starts to be directed. An electrical flow will start to stream when live terminals are put into the arrangement. The more salts that are broken up, the more grounded the salt arrangement and, correspondingly, the more electrical flow that will stream. This present stream is associated with uncommon electronic hardware that permits the cultivator to decide the resultant quality of the supplement arrangement.

The scale used to gauge supplement quality is electrical conductivity (EC) or conductivity factor (CF). The CF scale is most ordinarily utilized in hydroponics. It ranges from 0 to in excess of 100 CF units. The piece of the scale commonly utilized by home hydroponic plant specialists traverses 0-100 CF units.

The piece of the scale commonly utilized by business or enormous scope hydroponic cultivators is from 2 to 4 CF. (quality for developing watercress and some extravagant lettuce) to as high as roughly 35 CF for organic products, berries, and fancy trees. Higher CF esteems are utilized by experienced business producers to get extraordinary plant reactions and for a considerable lot of the cutting edge half breed crops, for example, tomatoes and a few peppers. Most other plant types fall between these two figures and the dominant part is developed at 13-25 CF.

Novice

At the point when a seed initially starts to develop, it is sprouting. Seeds are sprouted in a developing medium, for example, perlite. A few elements are associated with this procedure. To begin with, the seed must be dynamic - and alive- - and not in torpidity. Most seeds have a particular temperature extend that must be accomplished. Dampness and oxygen must be available. Furthermore, for certain seeds, indicated levels of light or murkiness must be met. Check the details of seeds to see their germination necessities.

The initial two leaves that grow from a seed are known as the seed leaves, or cotyledons. These are not the genuine leaves of a plant. The seed builds up these first leaves to fill in as a beginning nourishment hotspot for the youthful, creating plant.

Developing medium

Soil is never utilized in hydroponic developing. A few frameworks can bolster the developing plants, permitting the uncovered roots to have most extreme presentation to the supplement arrangement. In different frameworks, the roots are bolstered by a developing medium. A few sorts of media additionally help in dampness and supplement maintenance. Various media are more qualified to explicit plants and frameworks. It is ideal to inquire about the entirety of your alternatives and to get a few proposals for frameworks and media before making putting resources into or building an activity. Mainstream developing media include:

- Composted bark. It is typically natural and can be utilized for seed germination.
- Expanded mud. Pellets are heated in a hot broiler, which makes them extend, making a permeable finished result.
- Gravel. Any sort can be utilized. Be that as it may, rock can add minerals to supplement. Continuously ensure it is perfect.

- Oasis. This fake, froth based material is normally referred to from its utilization as a plan base in the botanical business.
- Peat greenery. This medium is carbonized and compacted vegetable issue that has been halfway decayed.
- Perlite. Volcanic glass is mined from magma streams and warmed in heaters to a high temperature, causing the modest quantity of dampness inside to grow. This proselytes the hard glass into little, wipe like pieces.
- Pumice. This is a smooth material that is framed by volcanic action. Pumice is lightweight because of its enormous number of depressions created by the removal of water fume at a high temperature as magma surfaces.
- Rockwool. This is made by softening stone at a high temperature and afterward turning it into filaments.
- Sand. This medium changes in arrangement and is generally utilized related to another medium.
- Vermiculite. Like perlite with the exception of that it has a moderately high caption trade limit - which means it can hold supplements for some time in the future.

Chapter 15: Periodic table of elements

Coming up next are the subtleties for building a hydroponic/aquaculture framework for your homeroom. I have utilized the mechanical assembly for as far back as six years in my group with magnificent outcomes. A 100 gallon aquarium fills in as our fish ranch. Groups of understudies screen the adjustment in biomass of the fish populace, (normally Tilapia).They likewise keep up records of the measure of high protein coasting fish nourishment expended. As aquaculturist they attempt to build up a taking care of system that will amplify the fishes development.

Science ventures

Water from this tank containing the fishes' metabolic squanders is siphoned at regular intervals through a progression of five hydroponic cylinders loaded up with basalt. Seedlings in Jiffy 7 peat pots are embedded into roundabout gaps in the cylinders. This soiless nursery can bolster around forty plants.We have developed numerous assortments of lettuce, spinach, herbs, tomatoes, cucumbers, jalapeno peppers,as well the same number of sorts of blossoms. In addition,climbing plants, for example, morning wonders or four o'clocks or nasturtia are developed straightforwardly from the outside of the aquarium by embeddings Jiffy 7 pots into coasting styrofoam. These are bolstered so they curve over the roof.

Except if there is a requirement for a particular photoperiod, lights are left on for 24 hours. Development is quick in the framework. A yield of verdant vegetables like spinach or delicate leaved lettuce is prepared for reap in around a month. There is sufficient time to permit every understudy in each class to develop their own yield and maybe time for some exceptional individual activities toward the year's end. We generally commend the gather with a pizza and serving of mixed greens party produced using the classes possess vegetables, obviously. While being used the framework can be utilized to outwardly show numerous significant logical standards from an assortment of orders, for example, creature and plant physiology, microbiology, and, obviously, biology.

The development subtleties are as per the following. The hydroponic cylinders are produced using four inch distance across, slight walled seepage pipe. Each cylinder is five feet in length and has roundabout openings 1-1/2 crawls in distance across, cut each six creeps with a keyhole saw. Jiffy 7 pots fit cozily into these gaps. The cylinders are loaded up with lightweight igneous rock which give incredible surface zone to root support. Plastic funnel tops are stuck to each finish of the developing cylinders . Delta openings are penetrated 1/4 inch from the base of each top and tee formed fittings are established into each hole.One half inch adaptable tubing associates each cylinder to a submersible sump siphon at the base of the aquarium. Flood waste gaps are bored 1/2 inch from the top edge of each top. One inch distance across tees are established here and associated by plastic tubing. This profits any flood to the tank.

A one-hour steady cycle clock enacts the siphon for roughly one moment, each half hour. At the point when the clock goes off, the rest of the arrangement will deplete back through the siphon through the fill line. A

24hour clock should kill the lights on and at interims that are proper for the plants being developed.

A thirty gallon aquarium or store ought to be adequate for this task. In the event that you have a business plant developing rack, a couple of disposed of aluminum bolsters make a fine superstructure for light help.

Materials and approximate cost
- 25 feet of slender walled plastic waste channel ($20).
- 10 feet of 1(one) inch distance across adaptable plastic tubing ($10).
- 10 feet of 1/2-inch distance across adaptable plastic tubing ($6).
- 6 plastic tees 1 inch distance across ($6).
- 6 plastic tees 1/2 inch distance across ($5)

Science ventures
- 2 tubes GOOP concrete ($8).
- 1 submersible recycling siphon ($80).
- 8 boxes of volcanic rock ($40).
- 1(one) 24hour on/off apparatus clock ($7).
- 1(one) 1hour consistent cycling clock ($60)
- Total cost = $242

Chapter 16: Tools and equipments required to grow plants in water

If you do not have a garden, it is still possible to green the living space with living plants. Arm yourself with the right planting tools and a little direction, and it's very practical to grow a beautiful nursery indoors.

There are a few things to think about growing indoors before focusing and soiling your hands: Indoor planting tilts because it has its benefits. Unlike the increasingly complex and increasingly complex outdoor garden, indoor nurseries are gradually attracting plant trainee specialists - on the grounds that you are not seasonally disabled. In a closed nursery, you can control the soil of your plants by controlling the amount of food, water, shade and light they receive. Plants currently grown in a cramped environment are likely to last more than one season.

Gradual: 7 indoor planting arms in case you run out of space For many of us, indoor planting works well. While mention is made of the UGA extension, supported by the authorities of the College of Agriculture and the Environment, we spend about 90 percent in recent memory. Growing a few great indoor plants can make your home state progressively relaxing and attractive, and it can benefit you when you develop something you eat. Indoor plants are also characteristic air purifiers that help ingesting indoor air pollution.

According to the National Gardening Association, you should see achievements in your indoor nursery when selecting plants that grow well indoors. The NGA proposes easy-to-understand interior choices such as glove, chives and lettuce, and especially herbs like dill, basil, rosemary and sage for starters.

When you get your favorite plants (or seeds), your hard work is not over. Being aware of indoor nursery requires normal consideration, but no one said it must be tedious. With these handy devices in the reserve of your tool, it will be almost all difficult to maintain plants.

Manual villa

For beginner plant experts who have no idea what fairies have to do with plant development, read carefully. The key difference between indoor and outdoor plants is that indoor plants may not have similar access to supplements. Adding manure and fertilizer to a plant-based plant can provide him with the minerals he needs - when disassembling reliable hand forks for soil and make sure he is properly prepared. Hand fork on Amazon. (Jewson Tools, $5).

Pruner

If you fondly remember Fiskars scissors from nursery, you are in karma. Fiskars also produces many adult instruments - explicitly aimed at improving the most massive indoor planting companies. Include a Fiskars PowerGear2 cutter, used by Fiskars creator and urban cultivator Russell van Kraayenburg, in an indoor planting tool box: A reasonable cutter offers a firm grip with extremely extreme impact for cutting stalks and light branches up to 3/4 inch thick. (Fiskars, $ 25).

Transplanter

Modest, solid and simple to utilize, it's hard not to adore the ergonomically structured Radius Garden 101 Ergonomic Hand Transplanter. The hand transplanter, planned with a patent-pending Natural Radius Grip to limit hand and wrist strain, makes it simple to accomplish the messy work without overextending or squandering vitality. This little person is best utilized for planting bulbs and transplanting to and from indoor pots. (Amazon, $16).

Mark creator

In case you're the sort that gets off on arranging, this apparatus is unquestionably going to explode your skirt. Not exclusively is a name creator amusing to play with, however it's an unquestionable requirement for indoor cultivating on the grounds that it helps keep indoor plants, seed bundles and supplies composed. The P-Touch name producer — called perhaps the best apparatus ever by Good Housekeeping — considers every contingency. Marks arrive in a wide assortment of tape hues with various text styles, embellishing designs and even nursery themed images like blossoms and apparatuses. (Amazon, $40).

Indoor watering can

You can generally rely on the Swedes to think of something imaginative enough to turn indoor planting on its head. Victor of the IF Product Design Award in 2010, Born in Sweden's indoor planting can is an affirmed work of virtuoso. The useful yet reasonable tempered steel watering can utilizes gravity to apportion water — basically move the metal chamber up or down to stop or start the progression of water. Utilize this one of a kind watering can to hydrate your pruned plants or to engage your companions at a gathering. (Amazon, $50).

Self-watering pot

This is the place the line among lethargic and splendid begins to obscure only somewhat: The new Aqua Camel is a self-watering plant pot that removes the mystery from attempting to make sense of how a lot and how frequently you have to water your indoor plants (regularly the hardest expertise to ace as an indoor cultivator). Dispensing with this under-watering/over-watering difficulty implies less dead plants on your hands. The licensed Aqua Camel pot, upheld by University of Florida horticulturists, is intended to give pruned plants as a lot of water as they have to remain hydrated for as long as 60 days, with no extra watering required. (Water Camel, $15).

Dampness sensor meter

On the off chance that self-watering pots are unreasonably cutting edge for your taste, and you need to adhere to the nuts and bolts of planting, there's a contraption for that as well. The Indoor/Outdoor Moisture Sensor Meter offers another approach to sidestep the regular issue of under-watering and over-watering parched house plants. The simple to-peruse needle meter has a shading coded check that mirrors a plant's dirt water levels, without any batteries required. (Amazon, $10).

Wi-fi plant sensor

For those occasions when you need an expert cultivator's touch, as usual, there's an application for that. The Koubachi (a.k.a., your "savvy" plant care individual collaborator) utilizes worked in sensors to screen the dirt temperature, dampness and lighting of indoor and open air plants. Using an iPhone or web application, this delightful little gadget that looks amazingly like a golf club will fill in as an immediate medium among you and your home plants — you'll know promptly when your basil needs more water or would favor a sunnier spot in the kitchen. (Amazon, $100).

Plant stand

When you have the fundamentals of indoor cultivating down, it's an ideal opportunity to consider introduction. Rather than swarming the entirety of your impeccably pruned plants on a windowsill or end table, you can sort out them pleasantly and perfectly in an essential issue in your home. An outline plant stand can be utilized inside or outside, with discretionary excited rack liners to get water run-off. Set up your plants on their racks, trust that the primary leaves will grow and praise yourself on a vocation all around done. (Planter's Supply Company, $80).

Chapter 17: Tips and tricks to grow healthy plants

One of the most common things that can happen in your nursery is the point where the plant gets sick. How could it have happened? Will it develop? Will my player eject a bin? How can I get rid of it? The most important thing in understanding disease avoidance is what many call the infection triangle (drawing, right). Illness can occur if three things come together: you have a plant that can get sick (host) and a pathogen (like parasites, bacteria, or infections) that can attack the plant and natural conditions (such as stickiness or dryness)) that advance the disease. If by chance one of these things is missing, the disease will not occur, so the prediction is to remove one side of the triangle. Instead of believing that this problem will arise in your nursery, believe that the best barrier to disease is a decent offense. Here are 10 different ways to get rid of each side of the disease triangle and keep your plants healthy.

Look at plants cautiously before purchasing great roots

The most straightforward approach to restrict sickness in your nursery is to abstain from presenting it in any case. Getting an illness with another plant isn't the sort of reward that any of us needs. Perhaps the hardest thing to realize is what a solid plant ought to resemble, making it hard to know whether the one you need is debilitated.

It is a smart thought to gather a couple of books, magazines, and inventories that show what a sound example resembles. Try not to bring home a plant with dead spots, decayed stems, or bugs. These issues can without much of a stretch spread to your sound plants and are at times difficult to dispose of once settled.

Notwithstanding checking the highest points of plants, consistently assess the root quality. One doesn't frequently observe clients doing this in a nursery place, yet it ought to be a typical sight. Spot your hand on the dirt surface with the plant stem between your fingers. Delicately alter the pot and shake the plant free. You may need to tap the edge of the pot against a strong surface to extricate the roots from the pot. Roots ought to be firm, generally white, and dispersed everywhere throughout the root-ball. Dull or soft roots are not a decent sign. In any event, when the tops seem sound, it's simply a question of time before a spoiled root framework kills a plant.

Utilize completely treated the soil yard squander

Not all materials in a manure heap deteriorate at a similar rate. A few materials may have debased adequately to be placed in the nursery, while others have not. Exhaustive fertilizing the soil creates high temperatures for expanded time spans, which really kill any pathogens in the material. Tainted plant flotsam and jetsam that has not experienced this procedure will reintroduce potential sicknesses into your nursery. In the event that you don't know of the states of your fertilizer heap, you ought to abstain from utilizing yard squander as mulch under delicate plants and abstain from remembering perhaps contaminated flotsam and jetsam for your heap.

Transplanter

Modest, robust and easy to use, it's hard not to love the ergonomic ergonomic Radius Garden 101 transplanter. A portable transplant, designed with a patent-pending natural radius to limit the tension of arms and wrists, facilitates irregular work without increasing your vitality. It is best to use this little person to plant bulbs and transplant them into and out of closed pots. (Amazon, $ 16).

Mark the advisor

In case you're the one bothering you, this device will undoubtedly explode your skirt. Not only is the name maker fun, but it's an indisputable indoor growing requirement on the grounds that it helps keep houseplants, seed packs and supplies under control. The name maker P-Touch - called perhaps the best Good Housekeeping device ever - takes all eventualities into account. Stamps are available in a wide range of ribbon shades with different text styles, decorative designs and even thematic images of nursery such as flowers and lights. (Amazon, $ 40).

Possible external water supply

You can usually trust the Swedes to find something imaginative enough to plant houseplants on their heads. Victor of the IF Product Design Award 2010, born in a Swedish planting bin, is a virtuoso affirmation. Useful but reasonable watering of steel can use gravity to distribute water - essentially moving the metal chamber up or down to stop or initiate the progression of water. Use this unique watering can to hydrate your pruned plants or hire your bridesmaids to gather. (Amazon, $ 50).

Self-governing the way

It's a place that attracts lethargy and a little darker glow: the new Aqua Camel is a pot for automatic watering plants that eliminates the secret of trying to understand how much and how often you have to water your plants inside. (regularly the most difficult expertise as an indoor cultivator). Giving this overflow and overflow difficulty involves fewer dead plants on your hands. The Aqua Camel licensed pot, supported by horticulturalists from the University of Florida, is intended to give pruned plants a lot of water because they must remain hydrated for 60 days without additional watering. (Water camel, $ 15).

Counter depth sensor

In the case where self-sealing pots connect unreasonably to your liking and you have to respect the nuts and bolts for planting, there is contraception for this. Indoor and outdoor humidity sensors offer another approach to avoid the regular release of odd plants underwater and overflow. The simple-reading needle counter has an encrypted control that reflects the water levels in the plant's dirt, without batteries. (Amazon, $ 10).

Wi-fi plant sensor

For those cases where you need the expert touch of the growers, as usual, there is an app for that. Koubachi (alias your partner in plant maintenance) uses treated sensors to check the dirt, humidity and lighting of plants inside and outside. Using an iPhone or Internet application, this wonderful gadget that looks amazingly like a golf club will fill up as an immediate intermediary between you and your houseplants - you'll know right away when your basil needs more water or hit a sunny spot in the kitchen. (Amazon, $ 100).

Standal

When given the basics of indoor growing, this is the perfect opportunity to consider introducing yourself. Instead of pouring your entire spotlessly trimmed plant over the window sill or end table, you can sort them comfortably and perfectly into the basic problem of your home. The factory stand exhibit can be used internally or externally, with a discretionary energized lining for the supports to expire water. Place your plants on their supports, believe that the primary leaves will grow and boast of your conscious call. (Planter's Supply Company, $ 80)

Additionally recollect that more isn't really better when giving your plants a beverage. Waterlogged soil or pots advances some root-decaying growths and can likewise choke out roots, making them obvious objectives for the spoiling parasites.

Try not to swarm plants

Trim out swarmed, harmed, or old stalks on plants that are inclined to fine buildup.

Swarmed plants make their own dampness, which permits illnesses like fine buildup to flourish.

Take care when separating transplants, and watch out for set up plants as they spread. Swarmed plants make their own dampness, which permits ailments like fine buildup (photograph, right), rust, and wool mold to flourish. Improving wind current around your plants decreases this high relative dampness and permits foliage to dry all the more rapidly.

109

Chapter 18: Selection and maintenance of plants

Front water layout

Landscaping along the coast presents problems that have not been encountered elsewhere. The powers of nature along the coast can be incredibly brutal. Salt showers, wind, poor soils, dry conditions, moving sand, storms and even salt water due to leaching will limit the number of plants that can be used at these destinations. These components spoil many plants of regular scenes. At the same time, the use of plant material may be the best technique for controlling the disintegration caused by coastal forces. Indigenous and naturalized riparian species are particularly effective, as they may require less support and maintenance. The attached information is intended as a manual for reproducing waterfront scenes and is also suitable for various destinations with dry sandy soils.

With any business along the coast, keep in mind that any movement within the property's territory or within the 100-foot cradle area depends on the department of the Neighborhood Conservation Commission which administers the Wetlands Protection Act (MGL Ch.131, sec.40), only as and all of the current permanent city rules. This mainly involves the licensing process. The areas of the property include bodies of water and wetlands as well as wetlands with fringed vegetation, coastal shores, elevations, salt marshes, seashores and salt marshes.

Plants and plants

When selecting plants for marine scenes, keep in mind that a pair of plants can withstand difficult conditions of complete and immediate presentation to the sea. Appropriate plant definitions, depending on the explicit conditions and the location of the site, become fundamental and essential to achieve any marine scene. Although the breeze and spray cannot be controlled, careful arrangement can reduce presentation to these conditions. Plants can be planted to house less tolerant plants. For example, the rose rugosa (Rosa rugosa) and the blueberry (Morella pensylvanica) can be used to erect a low and extreme external protection in territories other than the seafront coast. Behind this is a superb evergreen column , for example, Japanese white pine (Pinus parviflora) or eastern red cedar (Juniperus virginiana). When this screen is installed, it protects the least tolerant plants, allowing them to line up. Install screens largely with low materials on the windy side and a high breeze.

Regardless of salty and windy conditions, dry, penetrating sandy soils can also present comparative problems. An essential part of planting in coastal regions is the state of dirtiness. This does not only concern the coordination of coastal allocations or the inland areas beyond the coast. The sandy soil is dry and needs additives. When preparing the soil for planting, the expansion of natural matter in the planting territory is energetically prescribed. Fertilizer treated with soil droppings or peat greenery will increase the ability of sandy soil to retain water and additives. At least a 3 "layer of natural material should be installed throughout the planting area; more would be better. Trees and shrubs should be planted using appropriate techniques: planting openings should be three to several times the width from the root of the ball and not deeper than the estimated separation by the torch. in the storage compartment at the base of the root ball Discover the compartment compartment in the trees and plant them so that the flames are at soil level. Spell tolerance will require additional normal water throughout the main development season. Mulch will help reduce soil moisture and maintain cooler soil temperatures. Even with expansion natural materials, plants that are limited to dry sandy conditions should be selected as they will need less support and s oins after, we settle down. Plants that do not limit women will have the prerequisite for additional support and may be more impotent than insects and infections.

As a general rule, use local plants at all times possible. The best indicator of factory reasonableness will be the network of factories currently under development at the site. Current plants will tell you more about the location than almost anything else, and additional choice of plants can be made based on what currently exists. If only a few solid plants can be detected, for example, American coastal grass (Ammophila breviligulata), coastal plum (Prunus maritima), blueberries and red cedar, the amount of other reasonable plants will generally be limited. At different destinations with more asylum and better soil, even with water, the new blend of solid plants will reflect the largest number of choices available.

Grass grass (Eragrostis curvula) is a long-lived, packing plant that can be sown in sandy areas that is unlikely to blow sand. Firm to zone 7, it is suitable for poor, dry soils and has a large root structure that settles in sandy soils. It tends to sow at 5 pounds. per section of land on a delicate seedbed. Since it needs warm soil for germination, it is best to plant it between May 1st and June 15th and chop or sand it. Rolling or processing after planting to ensure excellent seed contact with dirt improves germination. Lovegrass will reset every time it is allowed to grow, along these lines strengthening the rest after a while.

Withers

In the strong reefs or territories where the sand blows, the American coast grass is the best plant to start planting. Coastal grass can be planted before winter and in winter until mid-April. The torpid tree should be planted 8 "deep, with several stems for each space, 12" to 18 "apart, depending on slope and presentation, such as thickness limits in endangered or threatened seabird environment (see Neighborhood Conservation Commission estimate Shrubs, for example, blueberry rose and rugos can be further used in climbs once the shoreline is laid, as coastal grass will protect the bush stalks from the depleted sand area.

Sok dikes

On embankment embankments, soil adjustment is incredibly problematic. Despite the fact that all the essence of the bank is vegetation there, groundwater leaks can dissolve or collapse entire segments of the bank. For barren shores, mulch, netting and decay covers planted on different seed grasses can be used to maintain the embankment until vegetation is set. Trees should not be planted on the shoreline as they should be used as they develop due to decay or strong breeze. Existing trees must be pruned. Grasses with their tough root frames will generally be better for balancing plants than shrubs. In any case, shrubs can provide shelter that will absorb considerable rainfall, thus reducing decay, and is acceptable if used in blend with herbs.

Any uncovered spots on the incline ought to be vegetated at the earliest opportunity to give a thick plant spread to control disintegration. Abstain from heaping brush or garbage on a bank as this won't shield the incline from disintegration and, sometimes, will keep settling plants from getting built up.

On the off chance that the toe of the slant isn't settled, the disintegration of the bank will keep on happening. At the point when segments of an incline are lost because of winter storms, waves, overwhelming downpours or wind harm, they should be fixed before extra harm happens. American seashore grass can be utilized to balance out the base of numerous slants yet must be utilized to the tide line. Biodegradable fiber rolls (bio-logs), with culms of seashore grass planted in them, can be utilized to balance out the toe of a bank, permitting the upper bank vegetation to get set up. In protected areas, salt swamp grass (Spartina patens) can be utilized in the region between mean high and spring elevated tide lines. Saltwater cordgrass (Spartina alterniflora) can be utilized in the intertidal zone. Both sea shore grass and cordgrass are accessible from business nurseries.

Gardens

The equivalent beach front powers that influence trees and bushes will likewise impact the strength of a yard. In poor, sandy soils, at least 6" of topsoil ought to be applied preceding seeding or sodding. This will improve conditions for good turf foundation just as limiting the potential filtering of supplements. Turfgrasses, for example, Chewings fescue, hard fescue, and crawling fescue should prevail over Kentucky country in any seed blend or grass mix. These grasses will have a higher resilience for dry conditions and a lower necessity for nitrogen treatment than country. Utilize a starter compost while seeding or sodding another grass. For built-up gardens, the utilization of a moderate discharge compost (for example WIN or Water Insoluble Nitrogen) will likewise limit the potential filtering of supplements. Water is vital for acceptable plant development yet light, visit water system advances shallow establishing of turf. Water gardens rarely yet profoundly, the soil ought to be damp to a profundity of 6" to advance profound establishing.

With an expanded enthusiasm for the utilization of local plants, numerous mixes of local grass seeds are presently accessible monetarily. Little bluestem (Schizachyrium scoparium) is a local grass found all through the upper east, particularly in waterfront zones. It tends to be found in blends in with fine fescues, just as blended in with tufted hair grass (Deschampsia flexuosa) and Pennsylvania sedge (Carex pensylvanica).

Local grasses can be left to shape a knoll yet will profit by yearly cutting to kill woody plants that seed in. On the off chance that cut grass is wanted, it ought to be kept up at tallness of 2 ½" - 3".

Cushion strips

Related to grass, a vegetated cradle strip ought to be kept up between the asset zone and the region of human intercession. A cradle strip can control disintegration coming about because of run-off falling over the highest point of and down a bank face.

Ways and walkover structures

Individuals consistently want access to the water; this frequently brings about individuals strolling down a waterfront bank or over a hill. If entrance isn't given by away, promenade or other option to proceed, the whole territories will be affected by pedestrian activity, every now and again bringing about extreme disintegration. To alleviate this, promenades or stairs ought to be introduced to close existing pathways that are causing disintegration. Passageways and edges can be planted with thick or prickly bushes to debilitate get to. Rugosa rose or ocean buckthorn (Hippophae rhamnoides) would be acceptable decisions yet any entrenched planting will work. Day off sand fencing can be introduced to restrict access in disintegrating territories. A license is required before any structure, for example, a stairway or footpath can be built. Check with your nearby Conservation Commission for prerequisites before development.

Conclusion

As majority of you realize I've been fiddling with hydroponic frameworks for a long time at this point, and it has been very fascinating to find its peculiarities and which vegetables develop better and which disdain it.

Of the plants that I develop, the ones that develop better than in soil are Peppers, Lettuces and Strawberries. Those 3 are basically all that I will develop hydroponically in future.

There are others that additionally become well indeed, for example, onions which develop to an enormous size, however as I don't develop for the show seat it is somewhat inconsequential developing football estimated onions for the kitchen. Carrots additionally develop well and with no root fly harm, yet you are confined to the ball type ones. French beans develop well as well, however in my set up I can just develop the diminutive person types and I very much want the climbing assortment. I would envision the diminutive person Runner beans would become similarly well, however I never attempted them. Cucumbers develop well as well however as they are climbing plants, I have a similar tallness issue that I have with beans

Tomatoes are an exemption. They become incredibly well hydroponically, and I have developed a wide range of assortments throughout the years and looking at them against similar assortments developing in soil. The hydroponic ones had more organic product per plant and greater natural product than the dirt grown ones, yet for each situation the hydroponic ones had next to zero flavour in contrast with their dirt developed kin.

That is likely the explanation most shop purchased tomatoes are entirely insipid as I would envision almost all monetarily developed tomatoes are hydroponic at this point.

The first published work on growing plants without soil was the 1627 book by Sylva Sylvarum by Francisco Bacon. Aquatic culture quickly became a popular research technique after its publication, but it wasn't until the 1920s that the idea really took hold.

In 1929, William Frederick Gericke of the University of California at Berkeley began to promote the idea that a solution crop could be used for agricultural production. Gericke has successfully grown vines in his garden at 25 feet tall using mineral nutrients instead of the soil. Nowadays, this technology is used all over the world.

The use of hydroponic plant production technology has many advantages over traditional cultivation methods. In hydroponics, the plant roots have constant access to an unlimited supply of oxygen, as well as access to water. This is especially important because it is a common mistake when you grow too much or too little food. Hydroponics eliminates this margin of error by controlling the amounts of water, mineral salts and oxygen.

Other benefits of hydroponic technology include the ability to better control plant nutrition, a noticeable improvement in quantity and yield, shorter growth intervals for many plants, high propagation success rates, savings in , the absence of pesticides and herbicides and more efficient use of space. As the world's population continues to grow, it is the last point that makes technology so useful.

Hydroponics can potentially feed a large part of the world's population and allow Third World countries to feed their own populations, even in places where the soil is poor and water is scarce. This technology can also be used as a valuable source of food production in places where space is scarce.

In Guangzhou, China, 14 roof containers of 1,600 square feet are installed, producing hundreds of pounds of vegetables each year. The tanks are part of a study that tries to show residents and developers in a Chinese city that their roofs can create a regular supply of vegetables that is even cheaper than the alternatives purchased at the store. Published in the journal Agronomy for Sustainable Development in July, the results of the study describe a comprehensive business model for hydroponic rooftop farming, a method already used in the United States, Canada and Europe.

By 2020, Guangzhou's population is expected to almost double, from 9.62 million in 2010 to 15.17 million. With this growing population, there is also a need to produce more food, create jobs and reduce the carbon footprint of transporting food to cities.

Quoted by Quartz, a research associate at the Worldwatch Wanquing Zhou Institute: "Roof trusses are necessary not only in Chinese cities but also in all major cities that have resources (roof spaces, water, sunlight) who still rely heavily on food produced over long distances. "

The ability to grow and produce food in urban cities eliminates the carbon footprint created by transporting food from rural areas to urban centers. Across the Pacific, the cities of New York, Chicago and Montreal have achieved some success with hydroponic rooftop farms. Gotham Greens has four hydroponic greenhouses on rooftops in New York and Chicago, which produce leafy greens, herbs and tomatoes. Canadian company Lufa Farms was recognized for opening its first commercial greenhouse on the roof in 2011 and now has a second greenhouse in the city, producing 120 tonnes a year.

As consumer demand for sustainably produced and sourced food continues to grow, hydroponic rooftop farms like these in North America are expected to continue to appear in cities around the world. Rapid urbanization in countries such as China and the consequent reduction of land available for agricultural activities will force people to come up with new ideas and technologies to meet the needs of the larger population in smaller spaces.

The advancement of hydroponic technology since Gericke first promoted the idea has made landless agriculture possible in urban areas. This simple but effective method is essential to address the issue of sustainable food supplies as the world's population continues to grow.

For anyone in the UK who wants to try technology, Ikea introduced a range of garden hydroponic gardening products as part of the Krydda / Växer collection earlier this year.

The Ikea website says, "Anyone can grow a garden," and the collection contains everything you need to put your fingers in the green and start growing your own herbs and lettuce.

With a world population of almost 7.5 billion people and global prosperity and the desire for food too rich in resources to grow too much, it is clear that agriculture must become more productive.

One way to meet future food needs could be to grow hydroponics: cultivate landless plants, instead of using nutrients with nutrient solutions to provide water and minerals to the roots. While it sounds like science fiction, it's not new.

The Aztecs built farms around the island town of Tenochtitlan, and explorer Marco Polo wrote that he had seen floating gardens during his travels to China in the 13th century. In the 1930s, Pan American Airways established a hydroponic farm in the distant Pacific Ocean so that it could supplement its flights with food traveling to Asia.

In conventional agriculture, the soil supports the roots of the plant, helping it stay on its feet by providing it with the nutrients it needs to grow. In hydroponics, plants are artificially supported and a solution of ionic compounds provides nutrients instead. Managing and maintaining a hydroponic system can be complex. Plants need dozens of essential nutrients, the optimal amount of each variable depending on the type, growth phase and local conditions, such as water hardness.

In addition, certain compounds react with each other and form substances which are more difficult to absorb and must therefore be supplied separately. Hydroponic producers must have a good understanding of the interaction of plants and nutrients and must monitor their solutions carefully and react to any change in concentration.

Farmers must also protect their nutrient solutions from contamination by unwanted substances. Closing hydroponic systems in buildings or greenhouses is a common way to avoid pollution of plants. Hydroponics can also control and optimize other environmental impacts on plant growth such as temperature, light and CO_2 and further increase yields.

What is hydroponics?

In theory, hydroponics can be used to grow any type of plant. However, the technique is mainly used with plants that grow effectively in hydroponic conditions, such as lettuce, cucumber, pepper and herbs. It is most commonly used for growing tomatoes in hydroponics.

Examples of hydroponic treatment In 2013, Thanet Earth, the UK's largest greenhouse complex, based in Kent, used hydroponics to produce around 225 million tomatoes, 16 million peppers and 13 million cucumbers, or 12, 11 and 8%, respectively. annual production of these crops in Great Britain. It currently manages four greenhouses and plans to build three more.

Globally, the hydroponic agriculture sector was estimated at $ 21.4 billion in 2015, with an estimated growth rate of 7% per year. Agriculture seems to be evolving slowly but persistently.

But similarly, major global changes are on the horizon that could dramatically accelerate the use of controlled agriculture in the environment. By 2050, an additional 3 billion people could live on Earth, with more than 80% of the world's population living in urban centers. We already use the vast majority of land suitable for crop growth, so new growing areas have to be found, especially in arid regions.

Vertical urban farming is an extremely controversial solution - the creation of complex hydroponic farms inside buildings, including tall skyscrapers. This would solve the problem of the exhaustion of available agricultural land and the creation of farms where crops are needed - our densely populated cities of the future. Vertical farms have already been built in Michigan and Singapore - and even in abandoned air shelters in south London.

And while it designs human space missions that will travel farther and farther from Earth, NASA is studying whether hydroponics can be used to create space farms to feed astronauts. Working with the University of Arizona, he sees if he can create a closed loop system that brings human waste and CO_2 to a hydroponic farm to produce food, oxygen, and water. .

The population is increasing, the land used is getting smaller and hydroponics can help us solve some future problems!

CPSIA information can be obtained
at www.ICGtesting.com
Printed in the USA
LVHW080804070121
675391LV00035B/12